REAL PROPERTY, REAL PROFIT

Laurie Duncan

Real Property, Real Profit: The REAL Way to Create a Monster Property Business by Laurie Duncan.

First edition published in Great Britain in 2025 by Extremis Publishing Ltd., Suite 218, Castle House, 1 Baker Street, Stirling, FK8 1AL, United Kingdom.
www.extremispublishing.com

Extremis Publishing is a Private Limited Company registered in Scotland (SC509983) whose Registered Office is Suite 218, Castle House, 1 Baker Street, Stirling, FK8 1AL, United Kingdom.

A CIP catalogue record for this book is available from the British Library.

ISBN: 978-1-0682314-5-2

Typeset in Merriweather.

Printed and bound in Great Britain by IngramSpark, Chapter House, Pitfield, Kiln Farm, Milton Keynes, MK11 3LW, United Kingdom.

REAL PROPERTY, REAL PROFIT

THE REAL WAY TO CREATE A MONSTER PROPERTY BUSINESS

Laurie Duncan

eXtremis publishing

CONTENTS

REAL PROPERTY, REAL PROFIT

Laurie Duncan

INTRODUCTION

About Us

The coolest thing for me about writing this book, is that there's a high probability that you've never even heard of us. Hope the catchy title drew you in! That's one of the reasons I wanted to write this (what is now our second) book! So now, of course, you need to go and check out our first book too – *Fast Track to Property Millions.* You can get that on Amazon and Audible, as you prefer.

Honestly, before we wrote that last book, we didn't have a clue about how to write, what to write, the process, etc. We didn't even really know why we wrote the book, apart from trying to get ourselves out there a bit more, a bit of marketing and a bit of credibility. As everybody knows, once you've written a book, you're more credible! Right?! Well, maybe we still don't have a clue, but what we do have is another two years' experience from last time, and an abundance of knowledge and experience to share. And I guess, since this is our second book, we are now "Proper Authors"!

Although this book is being written by me, Laurie Duncan, it is based around business experience of working in REWD (REAL Estate WEALTH Development) Group (or REAL Property Scotland, as we've become better known recently), together with Alex Robertson and Conar Tracey. All three of us fully appreciate each other, and there is absolutely no doubt that we wouldn't be doing what we are – in business and in life – if it wasn't for each other. I'd like to take this opportunity to give a bit of kudos to these two massively influential guys – both so uniquely talented, driven, creative and determined – as I cannot imagine my life without you. We are doing so many cool things together and I never want that to change.

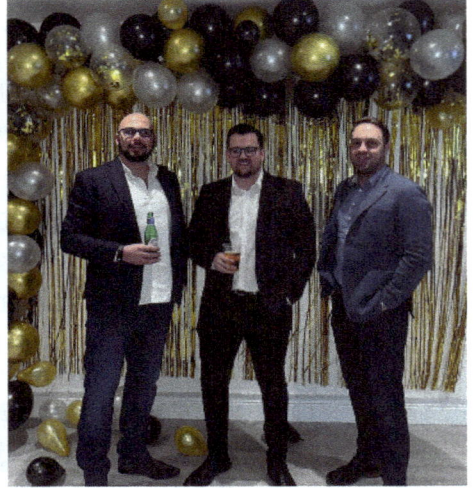

With the above said...! I am indeed married (no, not to Alex and Conar, but) to my totally super-awesome wife, Emma. And as much as I love Alex & Conar, I will never love them the same way I love Emma. I'm sure you can understand! Emma has been by my side since 12th October 2007, when we first got together. We were married on 4th August 2018, and since then have had two beautifully amazing kids: Daniel (2020) and Chloe (2022).

Emma has been through absolutely everything with me – there's nothing we've not done together. We have created such a sensational lifestyle together, and again, I would simply not be able to be doing what I am if it wasn't for Emma's continual love, support, and belief in me, even when some of my ideas are proper off-the-scale wild! Love you forever Emma – you make me smile.

Where I tend to be the motivational guy, the big dreams guy and the finance guy, and Alex tends to be the analytical guy, the accountant guy and the systemisation guy, Conar remains the deal machine guy, as well as bringing sales, marketing and general management experience to the table. Whilst Alex and I came from oil and gas corporate backgrounds, Conar has always been involved in property trading since the early days of his career, and has vast experience in estate agency, auctions and off-market property sourcing. We are a formidable team, and our results in business speak for themselves.

I also must make it clear that the name of REWD was really cool and funky as we started off our journey, but we moved away from the word (since it sounds like "rude") because it got a little bit weird for us the more we grew. So as I talk many times throughout this book about "REWD Group", we have actually transitioned away from that name towards "REAL Property", which is the name of our main trading entity within the Group of companies. After discussing internally, it was clear we were REAL guys, REAL investors, producing REAL deals and REAL results, for all our REAL clients – so the word "REAL" was the right word for us to move forward with.

We've always been open, honest and legitimate in our approach to business. In contrast, there's a tonne of fakes and sharks out there that will take you to the cleaners if you're not careful! A lot of "training companies" with no substance behind their social media rhetoric. We know people out there offering education and support services, but they've never bought a property deal themselves. Some of them rent their place of residence too, so they've never even bought their OWN home! It baffles me. Just be careful out there – we want to see you succeed.

GOODBYE REWD.

REAL Property Scotland

485 views • 15 hours ago

Our Start-up Story

So where did it all begin...?

We agreed a £25K purchase on a 2-bed, 4-in-a-block ex-local authority flat in Alloa. Alex got the lead, I negotiated with the vendor, and we agreed to buy (before having any idea as to how we were going to fund it)! Bizarrely, the lead came from a £50 boosted post from Alex on Facebook. We set up a new company and agreed to split any profits 50/50, whatever that actually looked like – we didn't really know if we would hold it as a BTL or sell it on for a profit, at that stage. Again, a low value property, so we couldn't get a "mortgage", but also this one had to be cash regardless due to a necessarily quick turnaround time. We were speaking to one of our mates, just by chance (yeah sure – just by chance)! I'll talk about "POTFU" later in the book – take a mental note of that terminology for now. Anyway, our mate had exactly £25K in his bank doing absolutely nothing, and he was keen to earn a bit of interest from it. We gave him a 1st Charge Security, paid for the refurb on a credit card, let it out for £550pcm, and refinanced it at £65K around 8 months after we bought it. The end result was a "free" property, as we extracted all cash invested, plus some additional cash, had created a decent equity position, AND we were cash flowing through rental income. We ended up keeping it as a BTL property, and that was our first ever deal together. At the time, the company was called "We Buy Properties Scotland Limited".

Second deal, it was a vice versa situation – I got the lead, and Alex negotiated with the vendor. We agreed to buy the deal for £60K, with a home report at £120K. Again, we'd no idea how to fund it, but believed in ourselves to get the job done! We brought in another private investor (a guy that Alex used to work with), he funded the £60K for purchase, and then we stuck the £15K refurb on a credit card again. The refinance of this one was not straightforward, and in fact it nearly (and could have!) sunk us. We got a dodgy valuation at the initial refi of £80K, which meant we were leaving circa £20K in this deal. If it wasn't for our determination to continually create solutions from whatever problems came up, we might have had a different story to tell about this part in our journey. Thankfully, we don't, and the same property refinanced another few months down the line at a £110K valuation in our first portfolio refinance. This meant at this point that we got all the cash out of the deal plus a little extra.

After those initial two, we decided to level up, as we could see how – by simply repeating this process – we would quickly build up a decent portfolio, and in fact that's what we did. But for our third acquisition, we decided to take on our first HMO project – 8 Union Road in Grangemouth. There's a long story on this one, involving industry sharks, a nine-day legal settlement, private finance coming from Spain, the HSE, and various other things…!

But the important part was, as usual, we got the job done. A little further down the line we purchased 14 Union Road, right across the hall from number 8, and did the same thing in there. Now we have them on long term lets, and each property nets us around £3.5K pcm cashflow. Again, there's a bit more to the full stories here, but the end result was why we took on the projects, and now we are reaping the rewards.

We ended up getting to around forty units within the first eighteen months of working together. Our plans had come into effect nicely, but we wanted more. Looking at the expansion of the business to that point, it was clear that if we simply continued down that path, we would have many more units, keep expanding, could leave our jobs, and go and play golf every day! The golf thing sounds appealing at first, but I think for any true entrepreneur, you're always looking for that next opportunity. I know for a fact if we just sold up and moved into early retirement, I would last about a month before I started looking for the next wave of business.

We wanted to MASSIVELY scale, and I mean to have hundreds of properties in a short period of time – not just tens of properties. The logical thing for us to do was to start buying portfolios (as well as continuing to buy single units). The problem was, we'd never purchased a portfolio before, but we decided it was time to learn. Then, as it happened, the first portfolio we purchased was an 82-unit portfolio across Central Scotland, valued at £3.7m. We purchased these units for £2.9m (a 20% discount from AMV), and created day one cashflow due to a rent roll of £35K per month. Back in October of 2020, this purchase was our largest acquisition to date at that time in terms of value, number of units, and rent roll. I guess in true REWD style, we went a bit gung-ho, and we pulled off a result that most would've shied away from because it was "too scary". As with every deal, that acquisition was not without its challenges, but we got it done, and that's all that matters.

Our Track Record

One of the main things that baffles me about these "gurus" you see online, is that they very rarely talk about the size of their own portfolio, or the rental income, or the deals they're doing, or any other more in-depth specialist knowledge of business generally. We've always been really open with absolutely every aspect of our business, because we are genuine in our approach to help others achieve results for themselves and we want people to see that we've been through "all the shit" ourselves! So the track record speaks for itself – at the time of writing (first half of 2025), we currently own around 350 units with an asset value of £25m+, and that's just on our residential BTL portfolio. On top of that, we have multiple trading businesses, including:

- REAL Property Scotland

  - Education, support, ongoing accountability & mentorship,

  - Off-market deal sourcing & trading,

  - Estate agency,

  - Property auctions, and

  - Project Management of client refurbishments.

- REWD Developments

  - Initially created for larger scale projects, commercial conversions, land development,

  - Now focuses on residential flips and auction trades.

- REWD Black Loch Limited

  - Holiday resort development project to form 12 lodges, restaurant, café, kids' playpark and over 100 car parking spaces,

  - We have recently decided to sell this site, and at time of writing it is now on the market.

It's important to mention that we do not offer any of our support services externally. These businesses only provide additional support to our investor clients working with us on the mentorship side. We have dabbled with external activity in the past, but we are now laser-focused on ensuring massive success for our clients, and so we keep everything we offer just for them.

For the paperback version of the book, I've added our portfolio growth charts as images. For the audiobook version, I obviously can't show them here very easily, but if you just email me directly, I'll send you the diagrams by reply – and, as you'll find, they are quite cool to see. My email address is **Laurie.Duncan@realpropertyscotland.co.uk**. (Let me know what you thought of the book too while you're at it!) We like the fact that we are very approachable, whereas many of these other "Training providers" seem to aggressively distance themselves from interaction with their potential customers. I don't consider us to be "Training providers", to be fair, but we are often pigeonholed into that category. Personally I think the distancing is a bit weird! And I like to get to know our clients, so I love the one-on-one communications. Email me, DM me on social media, or send me a postcard to REAL HQ! Then, I hope one day we can hang out and enjoy cocktails together at the quarterly client meet-ups. Mine's an espresso martini when you're ready.

Growth charts are shown on the next page, to give you an idea of our initial scaling phase, noting these were from back in the day and only take us up to December 2020. I actually stopped mapping them out at that point, as we were continuing to buy more, then selling some, then doing bigger deals, etc., and the admin was becoming a bit of a nightmare. The "Aberdeen x100" deal concluded in September 2024 – our biggest deal to date – and this took us to over 300 units; currently we are sitting on around 350 units in the middle of 2025.

RENTAL INCOME

TOTAL NO. UNITS

TOTAL ASSET VALUE

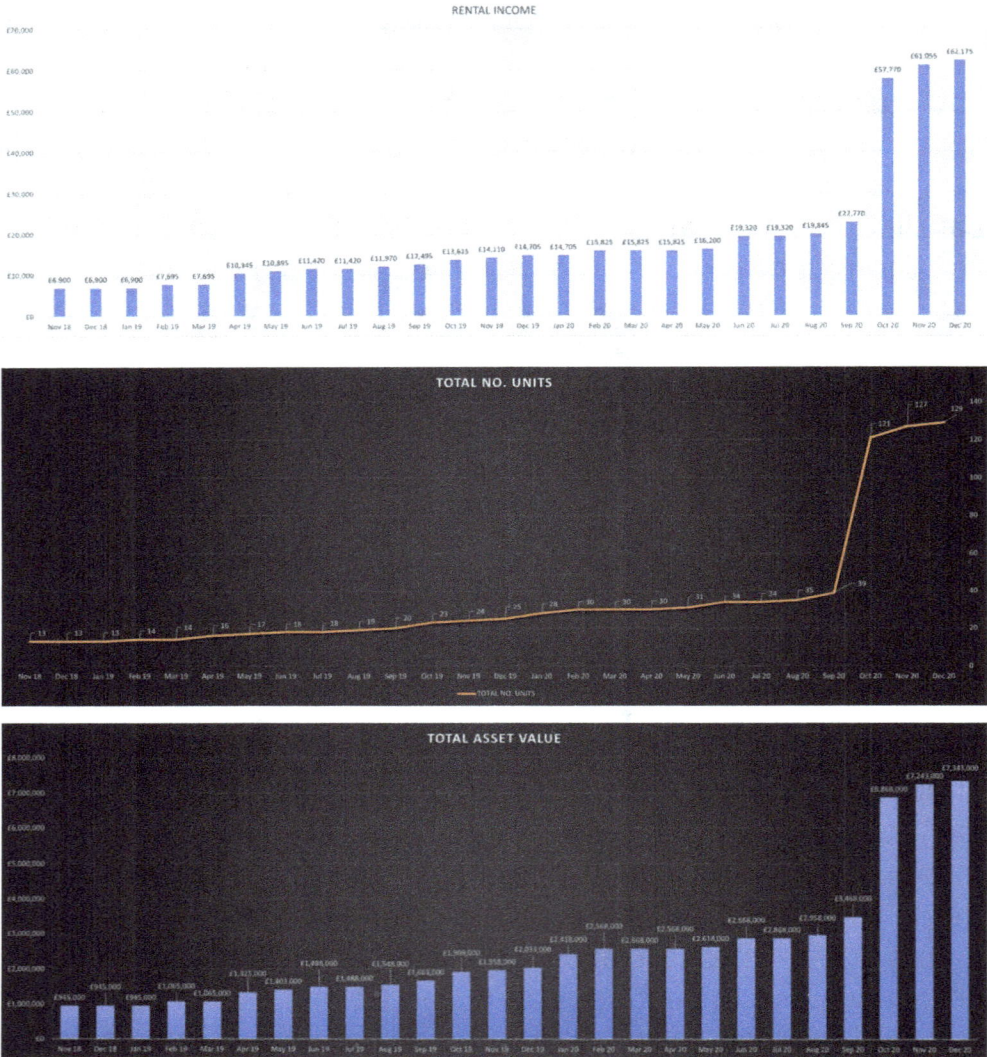

I think it's also really important to bear in mind that we've built up the Group in its entirety with none of our own money. Currently we have a round £4m in play with OPM (Other Peoples' Money). It's one thing analysing the track record of the number of units, rental income, asset value and equity position, but there's also been a solid track record of raising finance for us.

Not that we wouldn't necessarily know about other new businesses that have started up and raised this amount of capital, but I'm just not sure anybody has actually ever achieved what we have in the short space of time we've been going. If they have, I would love to know about them and go for a beer together! Obviously there could be situations with a start-up business where a venture capitalist backer has made a cash injection to get things up and running from the start, but that's not what we did. We have continually raised cash from various different methods of creative finance solutions such as private investors, pension funds, credit cards, commercial funders, and equity release (amongst others). It's a feat on its own merits, never mind all that we've done with the property side of our operations. Raising finance is a skill – master that, and you can buy as many properties you want.

Our Businesses

We started out in buy to let. It gave us the "passive income" which allowed us to leave our jobs. Then, we had created a business that was providing us with income regardless of whatever else we had going on in the background. The freedom and flexibility allowed us to start new companies and put our focus into other ventures – that's what kicked off the building company, the developments business, and more recently our estate agency, auction house, and finance company. The finance company is effectively a bridging company, to fund our clients acquisitions at up to 100% LTPP (loan to purchase price), but we've not yet got that up and running due to issues in funding lines. That mix of businesses is what exists for us today, but I'm not sure if it will ever stop growing.

The final part of the jigsaw from our side, in terms of providing absolutely every service possible to our clients, is to bring a finance brokerage service into the Group, specifically for exit (or what is termed as "long term" finance) at the refinance stage. We have made some moves to explore this kind of opportunity recently, but as yet nothing has materialised. I imagine that we will see the addition of this revenue stream into our corporate portfolio within the 2025/2026 period.

There's an obvious question around why we don't have our own letting agency. To be honest, this question isn't going anywhere – we have a scale where it would make sense to do so for 1) revenue retention, 2) full control of our own portfolio, and 3) lettings for our Training clients. That said, there's a serious amount of admin, staffing, vehicles, capital, structuring, etc., etc. that has to go into getting this type of operation off the ground. Do we really want that headache? Well, not at this stage, anyway. We pay our letting agents around 10-15% of rent collected – it really is a small charge for the amount of work that they do, and means we don't need to think about it!

More recently we've been exploring increasing our commercial operations into the likes of B&Bs, guest houses, and hotels. From our side, we like to buy assets, hold for long term, rent them out, and collect the rental income. These types of commercial deals are really similar to the resi side of our business, so it makes sense for us to move into that space as a natural progression. I'm actually pretty confident that by the time I've finished writing this book, we'll have secured our first commercial type deal – if you follow us on socials, I'm sure you'll already have heard all about it.

But to get back to basics for a second. If you want to grow a property business, whatever the area you want to get into (and there's lots of different options, all equally lucrative!), you should focus on two things and you will go far in your journey:

- Raising finance

- Finding deals

We have become experts in both raising funding and finding the deals. The combination of these things, if we were to simplify our successes, is down to these two key skills. We can show you how to do both, professionally, if you want to learn.

Alternative Strategies

As we've grown, we've implemented or are exploring every strategy under the sun... BTL, HMO, BTF, SA, R2R, CMOs, C2R, Land, SARB, AS, Sourcing, CI, to name a few!

Here's a quick jargon buster section for anyone that doesn't know the abbreviations:

- **BTL** Buy To Let

- **HMO** Houses of Multiple Occupation

- **BTF** Buy To Flip / Buy To Sell

- **SA** Serviced Accommodation

- **R2R** Rent 2 Rent

- **CMO** Commercial Multi-Occupancy

- **C2R** Commercial 2 Residential

- **Land** Land Development

- **SARB** Sell and Rent Back

- **AS**   Assisted Selling

- **Sourcing**   Selling property investment opportunities to others, a BIG focus of REAL Property Scotland

- **CI**   Commercial Investment

For anyone who remains confused by any of these terminologies, stick them into a search engine with the word "property" and you will find the answer you need! And for anyone that wants to apply any of these strategies in life, reach out to me directly to discuss how we can help you create this new lifestyle you desire.

At REAL Property Scotland, as mentioned above, our USP is actually finding and trading off-market investment opportunities to our Training clients. We source properties direct to vendor (D2V) at considerable discounts against their actual value, as a trade-off for providing the seller with a quick, safe, guaranteed sale, regardless of the property location and condition. This is portrayed by many others to be a "quick-win" way to make some "fast cash", but in reality there is a hell of a lot more involved in being a professional property sourcer. Don't be fooled by this general marketing message from the world of "property training".

Mistakes

Now then...! Where to start on the "mistakes" thing? We have made so many. We've also had many (what most folk would call) "failures" along our path to date, and we will have many more too. We're OK with "failing", actually, as we don't see it that way. In our view, you can have "winning experiences" or "learning experiences" – just make sure you don't have too many learning experiences! So for us, we like to look at mistakes, or failures, or whatever other negative association you want to attach to the learning experience, as exactly that – a learning experience.

My old man used to say, "he who makes no mistakes, makes nothing."

Some learning experiences that spring to mind are:

- Overspending on refurbs
- Not having the "right" power team
- Thinking we could change the High Street
- Trying to run before we could walk
- Expecting everyone to have the same work ethic as we do
- Trying (although ultimately not regretting) to source deals ourselves in the beginning
- Buying deals that were not deals
- Spreading ourselves too thin with a real lack of focus
- Believing that you can go on a three-day course and come out of it a professional!

Regardless of all our learnings, it is a simple fact that we would not be where we are today if it wasn't for going through that process, in its entirety. So, all things considered, our overriding emotion is one of gratitude and admiration to our younger selves. We always had the ambition to "go for it", and now (like you hear many business owners say), we are so happy that we did.

It's always been a mindset thing for us. You will only ever fail if you stop. So, don't stop.

Our Model for MASSIVE SCALE

Many people wonder how it is even possible to do what we have done, especially in such a short period of time. I used to think this myself before we got started, when I heard about people making tonnes of money in property without ever owning any, or buying property with none of your own money, or making north of £100K on a single property deal within a matter of days.

One of the first books I ever read was *0-135 Properties in 3.5 Years* by an Australian guy called Steve McKnight. This was truly the very first baby step in my whole journey. I hate reading by the way, but I put that view to the side and persevered with reading through this book, page by page (albeit it was on an iPhone and not actually a paperback book!), as in all honesty I was too curious about the whole concept. This was the first time I heard about property trading, assisted selling, joint venturing, same-day flipping, etc. etc. I often think back to that moment in time where I decided to buy the book, and wonder where life would have me now if I'd taken a different decision that day.

Whilst there are so many varying strategies out there, both Alex and I always had BTL as our number 1 focus. FOCUS stands for 'Follow One Course Until Successful'. That said, nowadays since we have a diversified Group of property businesses, we have inevitably expanded into other things. But for us at the start, it was simple – we would Buy, Refurb (if necessary), Rent it out, Refinance, then Repeat that process – this is known as the BRRRR strategy. Raise some finance, attach that finance to a discounted property, acquire, tart it up as necessary, get it rented out for as much as we could get away with, refinance the property from its purchase price to its TRUE market value, and this is what would allow us to recycle whatever cash was invested into the deal in the first place. At the point of refinance, you create an equity position for your business (typically 25% equity if you take a 75% long term debt) as well as bring the majority (if not all) of your cash back to the bank account, to allow you to use it again in the next deal. Cashflow is generated at this point too, if it hasn't been already, and this my friends is the very simplistic foundation of buy to let, at massive scale, in a (very) short period of time.

FOUNDATIONS

Mindset

Without any doubt whatsoever, the number 1 thing that has got us to where we're at, is our mindset and our ability to see the opportunity in every single problem that has come our way… and there's been no shortage of those! So many people think that they can achieve massive results without any agro, and to be honest I can understand why, as well as sympathise with that naivety, as this type of crap is exactly what social media conveys to our subconscious every single day. Unfortunately, so many of us get sucked into this fictional expectation of how life will be and how easy business will be, and when shit does get REAL, this is why so many people fall down and their businesses or objectives fail, because the bump in the road was 1) totally unexpected and 2) too big to deal with mentally.

We've learned so much about our actions, behaviours, habits, nature, emotions, psychology, neuroscience, thoughts, feelings and most importantly how to bring all of this together to stay focused on and continually achieve what we set out to achieve – RESULTS! There's a tonne of different books out there that can be read as well as listened to, to educate you on all this stuff. It's fascinating to me that, although Alex, Conar and I approach things differently, whatever the situation, we have all ended up studying mainly the mind, when it comes to self-development. Our experiences in business have reaffirmed to us that in order to operate most effectively, we must, must, must have our heads in the right space.

Considering that it's typical for most people to train their physical muscles using weights or cardio or whatever other training methods there might be, why is it not typical for people to train the muscle of the human mind? Surely we need to exercise this muscle too − right? This makes such perfect sense to me, which is why I now make it daily practice to keep my head trained, learning, focused, switched on, and in as strong a condition as I can get it − I've found this to produce the best output by providing the best possible chance to handle massive obstacles and still achieve the (usually outlandish!) RESULT.

Personally, I now do so many different things, compared to my young, naive, narrow-minded self... I am now a version of me that my previous version would've been the first to rip the absolute piss out of − for being too "out-there", as a minimum. For being "weird". For doing things that most other people don't do. But I've come to realise, through trying out lots of different (and widely practised) tools and techniques, that actually it's the uniqueness that contributes so massively towards success.

How many people do you know that have a morning routine? Get up at 4am? Practise gratitude? Perform breathing techniques? What about regular intense stretching routines to improve flexibility and mobility? Exercise 4-5 times per week, first thing in the morning? Or practise the likes of meditation, visualisation and affirmations? Ever looked in the mirror at yourself, stared deep into your own eyeballs, and affirmed to yourself that you are capable of absolutely anything that life has to throw in your way? You like cold water therapy? Whether that be cold showers, ice baths, or cryotherapy at -75 degrees C? Perhaps a Shakti Mat session for 10 minutes barefoot? And maybe, even if you do know some people that will do one or even a few of these things, how many people do you know that do these things every single one of these things religiously? Well, again, if you were to tell my younger self that this is what my older self would be doing in life as he approached the ripe old age of 40, I'd have said to get out of my office!

For me though, allowing my mind to open up to the possibility – just the possibility – that some of this stuff might actually work, and giving it a try, has led my life down a path I once did not believe could have existed. If you've never tried any of these things, give them a bash. Don't you think it's interesting that we are discussing these tools & techniques under the "Mindset" section of this book? Success leaves clues, and I know a lot of other successful people that do this sort of stuff, so all my simple mind says to me is "well, if it's good enough for them, it's good enough for me, so I'm doing it!"

In September 2024, I lost my dad to his battle with cancer. It was a hugely emotional time for me and my family, and I cannot put into words how devastated we all are to have lost such an amazing man. My dad was massively inspirational to me in all aspects of life. He inspired not just myself and my family, but so, so many others. We were all completely overwhelmed at the funeral to see over 250 people come to pay their final respects – the busiest anyone had ever seen the crematorium. It was a beautiful ceremony – one that Big Pete would have been massively proud of.

My dad, Peter Duncan, had so many mindset-style phrases he used to say to me. He was never into the "hippy stuff" like I am today! (Breathing, meditation, affirmations, visualisations, etc...) He was a business owner though, successful in his own right, and taught me so much about both business and life. I'm going to rhyme some memorable phrases off here – I live by them; they've helped me so much, and I hope they can help you too, with a bit of jest involved!

He never took things too seriously, and always made a laugh and a joke out of even serious stuff – not to take anything away from the seriousness of any issues, but just to put a different spin on it, and it always made me feel much better about whatever was going on!

"Sometimes, you've just got to be tired."

"He who makes no mistakes, makes nothing."

"Carry on rewardless!"

"Be good, work hard, stay top of the class."

"We are all different animals!"

"No regrets – they will drive you crazy!"

And his trademark saying:

"If you worry, you die. If you don't worry, you die. So don't worry!"

At the start of 2025, I decided to run my first ever marathon, in memory of my dad. I've always struggled with running due to injuries and setbacks. I had an operation on my left knee back in 2017 to remove a meniscal cyst, and after that found it super tough to get back into a regular exercise routine, running or otherwise, as I would always experience pain in that left knee area. That said, I didn't let that stop me, and over the years I have built up a decent strength and cardio base, which has been the foundation to attempt the marathon run.

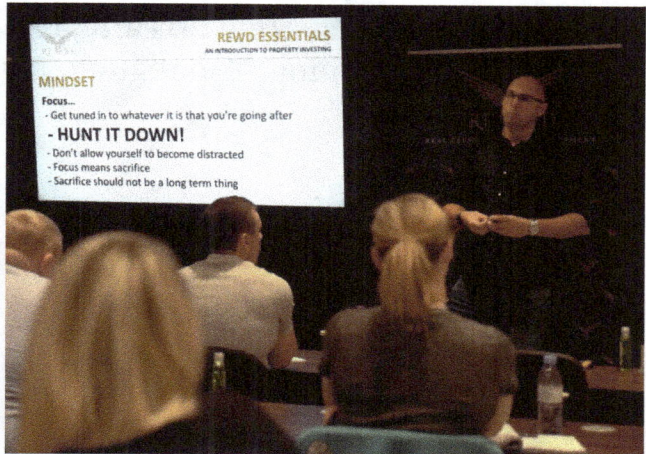

As is life, the marathon training wasn't going to plan, as there were always social events happening on Saturdays that would make Sundays a long-lie day, when I was initially planning Sundays as the "long run" day! In order to stay on track with the training regime, I decided to start doing my long runs on a midweek day, but to run 2.5 hours (around 20K distance) meant having to get up at 3am, to start the run at 4am, to be finished by 6.30am, to be back in the house for kids getting up around 7am, then would be time to get ready myself, to try to get the kids dropped off at nursery for 8am, and then I would head into the office after that.

Let's not kid ourselves on – and I heard this quote relatively recently and LOVED IT, so I'm going to use it here as one of my own favourite quotes, as it always gives me a bit of perspective when things are getting tough:

"LIFE IS HARD AS FUCK. THE SOONER YOU GET THAT, THE BETTER."

So…

I've always liked getting up early, usually 4am if I am doing exercise in the morning. The regime, for a few years now, has been:

- Up at 4am

- Gym at 5am (I have a gym at home)

- Stretch, sauna, steam, ice bath (also all at home), at 6am

- Get ready around 7am

The 3am thing was a change to the usual setup, but I immediately – after only doing it a couple of times – felt like I was addicted to this wake-up time! I know what you're thinking... 4am is ridiculous, never mind 3am! Well, I get it; I appreciate it's out of the norm, but that's also what I really like about it. I love getting shit done when the rest of the world is sleeping – it's so peaceful, tranquil, and a great use of time to get laser-focused on whatever I'm doing.

Initially, this 3am get-up started with the marathon training, but actually – even as I'm writing this section of the book – it's a Tuesday morning mid-February 2025, at 03:16... I'm writing this out sitting next to my daughter Chloe, who has also been up since 3am, since she's not feeling well. On top of me trying to write this book out, I am also being "superdaddy"; as anyone with kids will know, you've just got to crack on with it and "sometimes, be tired!"

So I started getting into the 3am club around start of 2025 too, and I honestly cannot see myself going back to the 4am starts, as I've now experienced a different way to approach the day, and get soooo much stuff done, before I even need to actually start the day-to-day goings-on of the businesses.

Now, why am I even going on about this in a book that's about property and building wealth...? Well, I've found that taking massive action, whatever that action is, will always serve you well. And if you always "do more than the other guy", you will go far in life. I go to bed around 8pm by the way. What's the alternative? Stay up in the evening, watching shite on Netflix, go to bed at midnight, then get up at 7am and go straight into the office? When will you fit in the tasks that will massive drive your business forward (like writing another book)?! Or when will you do your exercise? When will you get some "me time"? Just because society dictates a normal wake-up time, a normal time to start work, a normal time to go to the gym or do a workout of some kind, doesn't mean you need to contrive to follow that.

Be unique. Be you. Go the extra mile. Do WHATEVER IT TAKES. Only if you want massive success, of course.

Corporate Structure & Tax

Now, I must be honest, when it comes to corporate structure, tax, expenses, and all the other "accounting" type stuff, this is very much Mr Alex Robertson's bag. He is a qualified Accountant for anyone that is not aware, qualified by CIMA, the Charted Institute of Management Accounting. Having Alex's knowledge and experience at the table every single day, applied to property investment and specifically our Group businesses, is an absolute blessing. I've learned so much from working with this guy. What an unbelievably intelligent and clever man. And it's funny, like we all do, Alex now and again makes the comment that he doesn't feel like he's doing enough! As I have reassured him – just keep doing what you do, bro'!! For anyone that doesn't have an accountant in-house, I salute you. The value that Alex adds, is actually invaluable. No need to wait around for an external company / consultant / accountant to respond to whatever the issue is – Alex just knows, we can discuss, take a decision, and the point is closed off, allowing us immediately to move on to the next one. I can't imagine what business would be like without his talented, influential mind involved in all our operations.

That aside, there's some really important, fundamental stuff you need to get right to make sure you get things set up most effectively from the start. We will talk a little here about the SMART corporate share structure. If you're new to business, you've maybe not been exposed to the different ways you can structure your corporation. Very typically, a new business will be started with one Shareholder, one Director (the same person), and 100 "Ordinary" Shares at £1 each. These "Ordinary" Shares give that Shareholder 1) Rights to Dividends, 2) Rights to Vote as to the control of the company, and 3) Rights to the Capital value of the business. Now, when you're involved in residential BTL property investment, this gets very, very interesting...

Say for example you split the Share classes:

- **A**) Rights to Dividend ONLY

- **B**) Rights to Capital ONLY

- **C**) Rights to Vote ONLY

What this allows you to do is to push all future capital growth into a separate share category, without any voting rights or rights to dividends within that standalone category. As your business grows, the more units you buy, the larger your asset base becomes, and consequently (if you have not refinanced at all to extract tonnes of tax-free cash!), assuming your debt remains the same, you will inevitably create a MASSIVE amount of equity. Consider that in every deal we are doing, for our own acquisitions as well as our clients' acquisitions, we're creating £10-20K equity per unit. Multiply that up over even a small number, say 50 units, and that is an absolute MONSTER of a property business. Those equity values are day one at point of refinance too, by the way, so if property prices double on average every 10 years, as they have done consistently throughout history, well... I'll let you do the maths! But that's a hell of a lot of equity / access to future cash.

Ever wanted to become a millionaire? Relatively easily and in a very short period of time? Can you now see how simple that can be done in the property world? We can help you get there – reach out to me if you want to discuss. And by the way, you don't even need your own money either.

Anyway, back to corporate structuring and massive amounts of tax-free "passive income"...

I can hear all the tax experts grinning smugly because, at some point, we will need to pay the IHT (Inheritance Tax) on these monumental gains – right? WRONG! Not if you put your share classification for capital into a Trust. Don't worry if you don't know what the fuck I am actually going on about here – all this type of stuff is what we help our clients with. Don't get me wrong; we are not advising here, and you must always take proper advice from accountants, lawyers and other professionally qualified consultants, before deciding for yourself on the best course of action for your business expansion. Bottom line: there are lots of ways to legally avoid tax, if you set up correctly.

Frustratingly, the tax system is something that the government continue to play around with, to try to fix the deficit, as well as (I think) force entrepreneurs out of the UK – they're certainly doing a very good job of the latter. Over 10K millionaires left the UK economy over 2024, and it was around the same number in 2023. Government has always confused me with their serious lack of understanding of business, generally, and they don't seem to realise that if all the entrepreneurs leave the country, there will be no businesses that produce staff to contribute to the tax system. There's all sorts of global opportunities these days to set up and simply work from your laptop, especially in the tech space, so why would anyone want to lose so much of their earnings by remaining in the UK?!

We know so many people that have moved to Dubai in particular, due to the very aggressive tax regime regimes in that area – one guy in particular works simply from his mobile phone, and doesn't even have a laptop! It's incredible what can be achieved in this day and age because of globalisation and technological advances.

International tax residency is something we have been exploring more recently too. It's an interesting concept that can have preferential tax treatment due to the nature of the multi-country activities of the Group of businesses. Whilst we've not made any serious moves as yet, we are looking at expanding into the Spanish markets, for example, as a bolt-on to our existing auction house operations, as well as some other regions, and when your business gets to that size, the tax status makes sense to explore (as your initial country of startup, might not be the best country for you to continue in, as your main location of activity).

I can only talk from my own experience of doing what we have done or are looking into, but what I can say with absolute confidence, is that there is a whole other world out there when it comes to legally mitigating your tax position. I'll quote Mr Alex Robertson here, who has often quoted Lord Clyde's tax quote from back in 1929:

Lord Clyde, President of the Court of Session, ruled: "No man in the country is under the smallest obligation, moral or other, so to arrange his legal relations to his business or property as to enable the Inland Revenue to put the largest possible shovel in his stores."

I've personally never understood why people feel obligated to pay so much money to the taxman, when there's legal, legitimate ways to minimise what that liability is. The thing that very often separates the rich from the middle class, is that the rich understand the rules of the game and play that game to their advantage. If you were to try to explain these rules to someone with an Employee Mindset, they usually react with, in my experience, of statements like "that's a scam", or "if everyone paid their fair share of taxes we wouldn't have the deficit we do", or even "scum"! The facts of the matter are, they just don't understand the game. I'm not sure you'll find a business owner who doesn't look to minimise their tax position... Now, let me be clear, I'm not saying that there shouldn't be any tax paid at all

– maybe there should be, maybe there isn't a liability, it all just depends on how you're set up and structured.

Trusts, including International Trusts, combined with international corporate operational activity, can be a very interesting way to conduct your affairs. When the time is right in your journey, I highly recommend checking this kind of thing out.

I'm conscious, with all of this section said, that it might be overcomplicating things for a lot of folks, and that is definitely not my intention here. It's also important to note that the more complex of these structures I am referring to, are 1) not necessarily right for everyone, and 2) not necessarily appropriate for people starting out on their business journey. We've been in business for over five years now, and are now at a stage where it makes sense for us to consider more complex structures. When you're starting out, keeping it simple goes a really long way! And ultimately, in business, you just need to find a way to make

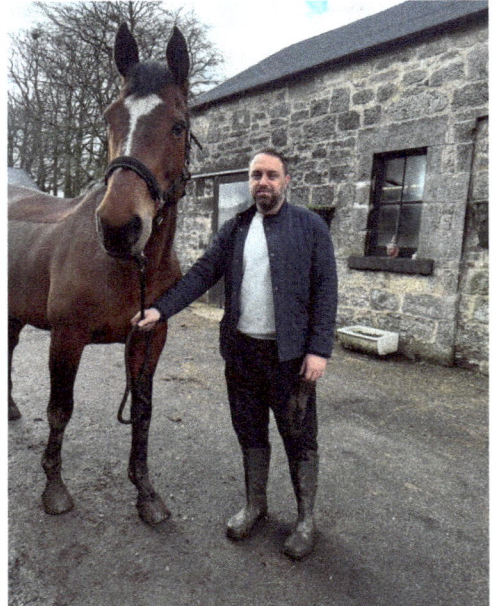

money, and keep making money, and make more and more money, to cover *alllll* the unexpected liabilities that WILL arise throughout the crazy bastard experience, and if you just focus on that in your initial days, and you don't become one of the many, many businesses that fail in their first year, then after that, it's then probably time to consider more advanced corporate structure and tax mitigation strategies.

Some seriously juicy golden nuggets in here though – hope you take them on board and enjoy!

Strategy

Since our inception, we've been totally biased on the BRRRR model – that's Buy, Refurb, Rent, Refinance, REPEAT! (Please tell me you've not forgotten about that already!) Of course, over the years we have applied tonnes of different strategies and monetised every one of them, very successfully. But as I alluded to earlier, in order to be successful, it is absolutely fundamental to FOCUS, and that's what we've done. Starting out in BTL is what created the "passive income" to allow us to leave our corporate jobs and focus on expanding the rest of REWD's Group activities.

Any time someone enquires about working with us, we always ask first – what do you want to do and why? Most of the time the response is "I want to create / build a passive income stream." So does everyone – right? Well, maybe not; it's not for everyone. Many people like the (quote unquote) "security" of being employed. What has become abundantly apparent to us from riding along this journey, is that you are either the entrepreneur who is taking all the risks and building the business, or you're working for the entrepreneur that's taking all the risks and building the business. Especially for start-up businesses, it's massively volatile. So the question is, whilst we understand that you want this "passive income", are you willing to do what is necessary in order to achieve that goal? Everyone, literally everyone, will say that they will, but the stats tell the story, that in fact only a very small percentage of people actually stay on the path to get themselves to the point where they achieve that goal.

Strategy includes anything that is a proven way to make you money in the property space. Whilst we have grown initially in BTL, we now regularly do refurbishment flips, straight auction flips, and seller assisted sales, all through our developments business. In hindsight, there's probably so much that we've missed out on, for going so aggressive on BTL, but at the same time I still believe that it's fundamental to get specific on something, whatever it is you're going after, when you're initially starting out in business. At this stage, it makes sense for us to consider these other strategies for our overall operating model, but when we were starting out, I don't think it did.

It's so important to build a foundation of 1) cashflow and 2) profitability (in that order)! I've come to learn so much about business, just from being in the game, but if you want to take anything away from this book, let it be that you MUST HAVE CASH IN YOUR BUSINESS AT ALL TIMES! No cash, means no trading, and that will literally put you out of business. Losses will come, it's a natural part of being in business, but if you don't have cash to trade your way out of whatever, that's that.

Clearly Defined Goals

If I think back to our initial startup and all the different Group companies we started up as we set out on our initial business journey, and think about the reasons as to why we started multiple companies rather than just focusing on the one operation – as is usually the case – with a bit of experience, we'd probably not have repeated the multi-company, Group style setup, had we started again.

However, it certainly taught us a lot, and we definitely wouldn't be doing what we are now if it wasn't for those moves we made in the past. That's the thing about everyone's journeys – they just wouldn't be the same journeys if the moves weren't made.

I think back now to our commercial developments on Falkirk High Street, as well as the building company where we employed around 30 tradesmen at our "peak", if I can call it that! Alex always takes the piss out of me, as one of my common statements from back in the day was:

"Even if we don't make any money from this, what a great learning experience it will be."

It is so, so funny to us now, to look back on that moment in time, when we were sitting together in Temperance House, which was an old empty office building on Falkirk High Street of around 650sqm in total size, that we'd bought as one of our C2R (Commercial to Residential) conversion projects, back in 2019. The whole situation around that moment in time is a golden part of our business journey. We started multiple businesses from that room of that building, and that's ultimately around the time we created the Group structure, including what is known as

REWD Resi 1 Limited (RR1). RR1 is what we termed as our "feeder company" back in the day.

Now, whilst there is no doubt we have had some phenomenal learnings, and we are much better placed in business and life now because of those learnings, starting out in business with a statement like that just demonstrates how naive I was back then, to think we could get into business and not focus on one thing – making money. It is absolutely essential to be focused on cashflowing revenue generation, as without cash in the bank you do not have a business. I'm very fortunate to be in business with two powerhouses of humans, by the names of Mr Alex Robertson and Mr Conar Tracey – Conar focuses on bringing the revenues in, and Alex focuses on managing the banks, cashflow, and financial projections.

Honestly, I often wonder what I even do on a daily basis, but the reality is that in business, there's just so many other managerial-type tasks that are required to be done, and that's what I tend to focus my time on, mixed in with a bit of constant analysis of the finance options out there, as well as the HR element of business, and continued efforts in a BDM-type role where I'm always looking to get our name and brand out there to see what opportunities might come out of the woodwork. There's actually so much admin to be done – even if it's just replying to emails and making phone calls – mainly to always make sure the magnitude of tasks and situations are continuing to move forward to the result, whatever that might be.

I have really struggled with self-doubt in our business journey so far, but have come to terms with the fact that it's actually quite a common thing for most of us to experience. There are days where I feel in a state of confusion for most of the day and find myself staring at the screen wondering what I should do next. There's days where I feel like we're knocking stuff out of the park for one reason or another! There's days where I feel super tired and really need to go for a nap. There's days where I feel like I'm on top of my game, and might randomly drop some inspirationally-motivational lyrical bombs! There are days when we do deals and they turn out to be sensational. There's days when we make a move and it just doesn't work out. All these things, I've come to accept, are just part of business and they're just part of life.

One of our clear goals is to become the UK's NUMBER ONE homebuyer, and we're are working hard towards this now, via our direct-to-vendor off-market "sourcing" brand of We Buy Homes Scotland, with our beautiful big mascot in the form of Hugh The Coo (to help you sell your home the noo)! Which basically means, in Scottish slang, we will help you sell your home fast ("the noo" meaning "now")! In order to hit that goal, we need to be working with buyers looking to continually expand their property business.

If we generate more investment opportunities, we need more clients to buy those opportunities, and I don't think we will ever stop expanding our buyer pool. Between individuals' criteria, such as property types, values, locations, etc., limited money pots per client (as most people tend to only use their own pots of cash, rather than raising more funds as per the finance section of this book – it always baffles me), and client cashflows, there's never any one time where we have someone sitting around looking for a deal and not being fed one. There really is so much opportunity out there in this market.

You hear a lot of folk talking about goal setting, and the advice is always to write it down. It seems such a simple thing to do! In fact, it is – perhaps obviously – very simple: write the words down. I know myself from implementing this technique when setting goals, from way back in the day and carried on to now; it is hugely impactful, and really does work. The best example I can give of this, is when Alex and I started out in buy to let, and the initial goal was 10 units. When we were edging close to that, we changed it to 50 units. It then became 100 units. THEN 300 units, before writing down for the first time, the craziest goal of ever (on the BTL side anyway), of 1,000 units. The funniest part about all these different stages of goals, for me, is that it kind of made me realise that we are entrepreneurs! We just keep changing the goals, making them bigger and bigger, and never really stop to think about how awesome it is we just achieved the previous one! This is a common trait of entrepreneurs, apparently. And it's not to say that we are never satisfied – I personally feel satisfied all the time, regardless of whatever is going on and what stage we're at – but it's to say that we are always pushing for more, to ultimately become a better version of ourselves compared to the day before.

I often reflect on how interesting it is that humans are humans. We, as a race, are such fascinating beasts. I really hope that you (yes, I am talking to you: the human reading this book right now) take on what I've said about writing the goal down. Be in the 1% - the 1% that actually listens to what others have said, the 1% that implements those teachings into their own lives, and the 1% that keeps pushing forward through all the barriers to achieve what the 99% will give up on.

Dreams without goals are just dreams.

MY WHY

Everyone has their own reasons for doing whatever it is they do, and we all have our unique inspirations for setting our goals. I've always wanted to create massive wealth, to the point that my family's families will never have to think about working, if they choose not to. Now, I don't foresee a life of laziness and sponging for my kids, or my kids' kids, and I don't imagine that's the type of personalities they will have either, given that they will have inherited the genes of Emma and myself, as we are both very hard-working individuals, but I would like our kids to be in a position whereby they do not need to worry about money. We will bring them up to work hard and not let anything stand in their way, if they want to go after any particular dream or ambition. I want my kids to be able to do whatever it is they want to do in life and not be held back or pinned down to a job they fucking HATE!

Man, that was me, for so long, and I think it's also true of so many others too. Most folk feel like they're stuck and just can't get out of whatever position they're in – I can relate. That in itself is a massive driving force for me in doing what we do now. Don't get me wrong, I learned a lot from my corporate life, and honestly I don't believe we would be where we are in business at this stage if it wasn't for going through a bit of pain in that time before Alex and I got into business. You need to have that type of experience in life though, I think, as it creates a situation where you realise who you are truly meant to be. I've always had this mad urge to get myself out there, connect with others, create something from nothing, and build it to something huge. I was always in a sales and BDM-type role, and so a lot of that stuff comes naturally to me just because I've done so much of it, and on an international scale. My mum has always said I'm good at dealing with a variety of people – I will get on with anyone of any personality type, and I guess that's a big part of what drives any success, just in terms of the ability to get yourself out there and mingle and suss out where the opportunities might lie.

If I think back to when I started out in my corporate life, I really never had a bean to my name. My everlasting memory is from my time at Canal Walk – that was my first house after I left my mum and dad's place – where I would live off around £600 of disposable income every month. I remember feeling constantly skint! I think around that time I would've earned about £2K cash in bank per month, which was around a £30K salary. I had a company car, so the benefit in kind came off that income – and of course, the good old HMRC helped themselves to whatever they were entitled to at the time as well. The mortgage was around £700, I had bills of another £400 odds, and then I had some other costs of the likes of credit card or loan repayments, leaving me with around £600 to play with. So often back then, I would be scratching around at the end of every month, trying to find enough money, somehow, to get back to the boozer every Saturday. That was my life back in those days – working month to month, zero money in the bank, no assets, proper skint, spending every weekend going out and getting completely smashed, hanging out in boozers, talking about and watching tonnes of football, acting like a weekend millionaire, and ultimately – when I look back on it now – completely wasting a shit tonne of my time that I could've used to progress my life in so many ways, whether that be professionally, in the property game, in business, in mindset... whatever! But I didn't. I was young, in my early twenties, and I did not have my head in that place at all. The overriding thought is more of frustration with all this, knowing what I know now, that I could've done so much with all the time I wasted. I get that it's all part of growing up and all that, but I do wish I'd started and focused on the property game sooner. Anyway, the point is – I was skint. And that taught me a lot too. It taught me that I never, ever, ever wanted to be skint again! And no way did I want my family to be skint. And that I wanted to live a life of abundance. And soon after that, that's when I started to screw the nut and settle down a bit, albeit focusing on my corporate life as my source of income.

So I started working in the corporate world, in sales for my dad's business at the time, which was a stockholding company for pressure piping products, supplying into the likes of the oil and gas, petrochemical, power, and offshore markets. I remember one point in time, vividly, when I was up around 3am to head to Edinburgh airport and get two flights throughout the day to travel over to Estonia for a couple of days for some meetings with clients and potential clients over there. I was walking through to the departures gate around 4.30am, together with another few hundred people – it was like a big snaking chain of humans trapped in their corporate ways. Most of the people were men, and most of them were grossly overweight – and I mean bellies hanging over their trousers, scruffy hair, wearing suits but not looking very well-presented at all. I genuinely could not believe what I was seeing, but it was an epiphany moment. There was me, walking along in this queue, with tonnes of other people that do this for work, day-in and day-out. I was about to meet clients for drinks and dinners, for a couple of nights in a row, eat plane food, eat airport food, do no exercise, likely with fast food for lunches, hotel breakfasts, have shite sleeps, then I suddenly realised just how tough it must be for these folk to stay on top of their health and wellbeing, when they were working and living away from their homes and their families. It was that moment in time – I can see the image perfectly – even that particular guy in the grey suit with the purple shirt and the big belly, it was then that I decided that I MUST change my life. I would not continue doing that job for the rest of my life, to not see my wife and kids, and sacrifice my health and wellness, due to travelling away for work all the time. And on that first flight, to Stockholm Arlanda airport for my connecting flight over to Tallinn, I did something I had never done before – I bought a book!

This book was called *0-135 Properties in 3.5 Years*, by an Australian guy called Steve McKnight. I bought it on my iPhone, and it was one of these books that you had to actually read (I mean as opposed to an audiobook, that I actually would've much preferred, where I could've listened rather than read), and I had to manually flick through the digital pages full of really small text. I was so curious about this title − I think I actually just searched something like "property investment" − and this was the one that caught my eye. And yes, before you ask, *Rich Dad Poor Dad* was the next book, obviously! If you've not read Robert Kiyosaki's book called *Rich Dad Poor Dad*, please (of course, only after you've finished reading my book here) seek it out − that is another absolute game-changer. Anyway, Steve McKnight's book started talking about how to buy property with none of your own money, how to make loads of money without even owning a property, how to do refinances, how all the numbers worked − I was blown away. This was the very first time I ever heard anyone talking that talk − it was a new language for me, but I LOVED what I was hearing. We're maybe in 2016/2017 at this point, and − with this new level of knowledge − I started on a path that has ultimately led me to where we are now in business, in life, in knowledge, in expertise, in experience... I cannot believe how stark a contrast I was as a guy back then compared to who I am now. I would never had dreamed of writing a book back then, never mind writing two of them! After I learned that I could consume an endless amount of knowledge from simply reading or listening to other peoples' experiences in life, I never stopped. I got into podcasts and audiobooks, listening to a wide and varied mix of property and business related content − hey, that's maybe what you're doing now! I learned so much in a relatively short space of time from so many books... but to be completely honest, that was really just the starting point. The REAL knowledge has come from putting all the learnings into action, which has created new learnings and opportunities on a scale that most would only dream of. I was a guy who would only have dreamt of creating the life that we live now. I really hope my story can motivate and inspire others to take that leap of faith. Break away from what you don't enjoy in life, and create a life of abundance for yourself and all the others that will benefit from your hard work too.

I never had a sheltered upbringing – I was very lucky to be brought up in a family full of love, happiness, success, music, creativity and business – I went on lots of holidays, globally, together with my mum, dad and four older brothers. My old man was the driving force behind my family's wealth, starting up in business back in 1978, and doing very well for himself through a hell of a lot of heartache and pain. I learned so much from my dad, in all things life and business – that could be a book in itself. But you hear so many of these life-changing gurus out there now, especially with the continuing rise of social media, talking about whatever the next hot topic is, telling their stories of rags to riches, transforming themselves, going from zero to hero – that just wasn't me. I had a great upbringing – my mum and dad

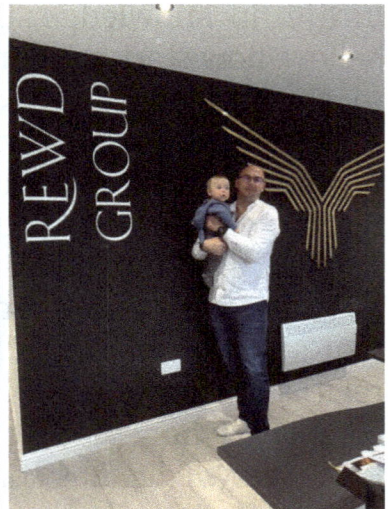

were really successful. There was no fluffy bullshit – just solid, hard work, that allowed them to create such an awesome life for themselves as well and my brothers and me. We are so fortunate and so grateful to our parents for giving us the life that we have now.

There's only myself and my oldest brother, Craig, that have actually gone into business for ourselves; my other three brothers – Michael, Scott and Jamie – have taken the corporate routes, and all do very well for themselves in their own industries. I guess that's quite interesting to think about too, as for me, I always wanted to follow in my dad's footsteps as I saw what business allowed him to create. I don't think I could ever have stayed in a corporate job, as I just knew that there was this whole other world out there and it was essential to me that I had a piece of it! Being in business for over five years now, I certainly didn't expect all the madness that new startups bring, but I tell you without any doubt whatsoever, as hard as it's been to get our business to the point that we're at now, I wouldn't change any of what we've been through – it's taught me so, so much, I cannot put it into words.

I always used to say to Alex right back at the start:

"All experience is good experience!"

and,

"Even if we don't make any money out of this, it will be a great experience!"

I have different views on the latter of those two statements these days, but I'm definitely glad we have learned what we have, so early on, on our journey, as it's put us in a much stronger and clearer position.

My parents, Pete and Irene, loved a bit of gardening. At the house we grew up in, Wallacerig, in Brightons in Falkirk, Scotland, there was a lot of land with the house, including what was known as "The Orchard", which was actually a mini orchard, full of apple trees mainly, if I remember correctly. I don't think there were any more exotic fruits, or any other fruits for that matter, and to be fair you couldn't eat these apples right off the tree, although my mum did use them often for cooking with. These apples also did not look very appetising! My memory of them is to always be a bit off-looking, usually half eaten by a worm! I do have fond memories of walking around there though, with our two dogs – our beautiful golden retrievers, Bill and Ben. That was a really cool part about Wallacerig – you could take the dogs out for a walk just in our own garden, with plenty space to run around and plenty of sticks to throw!

The orchard was sold off maybe ten years after my folks bought the house, as a plot of land with Planning Permission, for the construction of three houses. My mum and dad didn't want to get involved in the build, so they just sold the land to a builder. There was also a putting green, or so it was named, and we did have a little device for cutting the holes out of the grass so we could change the position of where we were aiming, but I'm not sure we ever used it as an actual putting green – it was just a large garden area, really. (I do think the folk that owned the house before my mum and dad might've used it as a putting green, or certainly further back in the past it might've been used that way.) But I mean, if you saw the size of the garden at Wallacerig, which they sold a while ago now – man, that was a full-time job in itself keeping on top of that! When I was a young hooligan, I would be out partying all the time, this was when I was maybe 16-24 odds, and my folks would always want to get into the garden on Sundays and cut the grass, do a bit of weeding, chop down trees, plant new flowers, trim the hedges and the likes. I, being my young hooligan self at that time, was lying in bed feeling rough as fuck from having been out all day and night, and wanted absolutely nothing to do with any gardening! My limits these days are cutting the grass and maybe watering my own hedge − the rest of that type of stuff, I much prefer to pay other guys to come in and deal with it on my behalf. They always do a better job, and relatively the cost is so low for what we get out of it!

Anyway, throughout this section, I guess I'm reflecting here again on other aspects of my life that have contributed ultimately to what is "MY WHY":

- My parents' work ethic and their own results of success in life. They showed me how to do it, and proved to me that I could achieve anything I put my mind to.

- My desire to create something HUGE, whatever that might have been. This feels like it's just "in me".

- My epiphany to get away from that corporate−style entrapment. If it wasn't for that experience back then, it might not have pushed me to make the moves I did.

- My beautiful wife Emma and our two amazing children, Daniel & Chloe. I want it ALL for them.

I think it's also important to write about the materialistic things in life that also drive me − no pun intended here! I've never been into cars, but always liked the look of a really nice one. The more we've done in business, the more I want an even fancier car. I currently drive a Range Land Rover Sport − that was my dream car since I was a kid. Growing up, I was always amazed any time I saw a really nice one. At one stage, I used a particular scene for my visualisation – that was me driving into the driveway, with Emma at the front door, with Daniel by her side, holding Chloe in her arms. I remember explaining this visualisation once to a guy I used to go to some of these personal development type events with. I think it was around 2020, and his immediate gut reaction was, "well that must be happening soon then!" I really wasn't thinking like he was, but he was basically making the point that because of the age of the children, in order for that scene to "come alive", it would have to be soon as kids grow up quickly! I hadn't even thought about that element of my visualisation. This scene came true for me in 2024. For anyone that's never tried the visualisation thing, I highly recommend it. I was previously the guy to take the piss out of this stuff. Now I'm a massive advocate, because I tried it out of curiosity, and it's worked incredibly well across so many different areas of my life. It is bizarre how it works – but it works.

Car wise, if I go back to 2020 again when we held our first live training event, there was a slide that featured a Ferrari F8 Tributo Spider as my ideal supercar of choice. I mean, to have built your business up to allow you to even be in the position to buy a Ferrari, even if you didn't buy it, man – that is an awesome place to be. I want to be the guy that gets himself to that position, financially, and to be honest we are at that point now, albeit I've not actually bought a supercar as yet! But that stuff drives me too... I want the fancy supercar, maybe supercars! I want the big house. I want multiple holiday homes across the globe. I want to travel First Class. I want to go out and eat fancy food and drink fancy wine. I want Emma, Daniel and Chloe to have whatever they want in life. I want to kick back in my recording studio and mess about on Logic Pro (which is Apple's music production software program), trying to create the next slam dunk of clubland for the upcoming Ibiza season. I want to travel in style, staying in fancy places with a butler and staff that will make us cocktails and cook our Michelin star meals, on request. I. WANT. IT. ALL!

It's so funny, but I really enjoy writing books. It's almost like a meditation for me now in some weird way – it's really fulfilling to think about life, all my experiences, and to have the opportunity to get it all written down here in the hope that it can help others get to where they want to be. Thinking of my own WHY, reflecting here, my overriding thought is one of gratitude. I am so grateful to everything that has happened in my life to bring me to this point in time – our story just wouldn't be the unique story that it is if it was a different story. I wonder if my family or my family's families will ever read this book, wondering where they came from and who was this extravagant character known as "Laurie LD Duncan"?!

For any of you that haven't yet made your moves, but can relate to this urge that's just "in you", I can tell you from my own experiences, the journey doesn't always make sense. All these mad POTFU experiences! (POTFU is Power Of The Fucking Universe, in case I've never covered that favourite phrase of mine yet.) So many crazy things have happened and I know will continue to happen, that I cannot explain. It's like thinking of the acorn growing into an oak tree – like genuinely, how the fuck does that even happen? Small seed, drops to ground, gets buried under some soil, it rains, there's heat from sunshine, it grows, day after day, week after week, year after year, decade after decade, century after century... this thing just keeps growing after these universal repetitions that nobody can really explain. It's just what happens due to repetition of process. Well, have a think about what you do on a daily basis and what result that is going to lead you to.

If you get up, go to work, work all day, go home, have dinner, watch TV, go to bed, then repeat that process, you will achieve a certain result. If you go to the gym multiple times per week, that will produce a certain result. If you sit around eating junk food and drinking sugar-filled fizzy drinks, that will produce a certain result. If you start buying properties and continue to build your asset base and income streams, that will produce a certain result. If you take X action, that will create a result of Y – you choose what you spend your time on and what actions you take. It's those actions that will lead you to the result of that particular path. Believe in yourself, and watch what these universal laws make happen – it is truly mind-blowing!

SYSTEMISATION

Power Team

For whatever reason, someone, somewhere decided at some stage, that rather than calling people "stakeholders" or "suppliers" of your business, that they should be termed something more sexy, and that terminology was said to be "Power Team". I've never really understood this – it's almost like someone is trying psychologically to make your suppliers sound better, or make it sound easier to achieve your goal by working with these people. Don't get me wrong: these people are absolutely fundamental to your success, so they are critical, and you definitely do require suppliers, just like any other business. But why they need to be called this strange terminology of "power team", personally, is something I've never understood.

Anyway...! Lawyers, accountants, letting agents, SA agents, refurb team, mentors, brokers, funders – yeah, basically suppliers – are contained within this power team. It's really important to get a good team in place from the get-go. We pissed about with different suppliers throughout the start of our journey, and made lots of mistakes along the way, before getting to a point where we now have a very good team of people in place to deal with a lot of our requirements. All these suppliers attract a cost, of course, but the relevant costs should always be factored into your deal analysis – whether that's front end for acquisition, during the refurb phase, during the exit / refi phase, or into the management phase.

The best thing about your power team, and I'll continue with this terminology since that is the heading for this section of the book, is that these guys will take care of the majority of the tasks

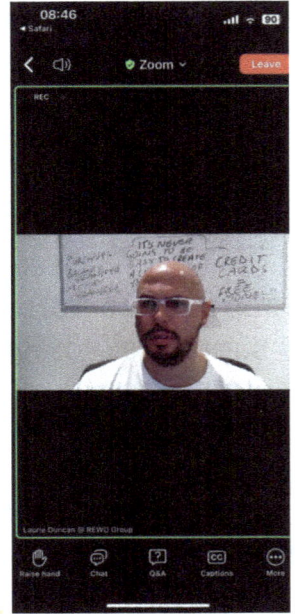

you require to make a success of a property deal. Really, you don't need to do much, apart from a bit of paperwork, sending some emails, some due diligence, then instructing your power team to act on your behalf, in whatever their area of expertise might be. So as you sit on the beach drinking piña coladas, these guys will be beavering away in the background getting your deals done.

I remember doing a deal over in Thailand at one point. The property was in Denny though, unfortunately, not Phuket. Emma and I were on our honeymoon actually back in 2018 – this was before REAL or REWD even existed. I was sitting in the roasting hot sunshine, having a look around RightMove to see what I could find, and battling with the glare of the sun on the laptop screen. There are deals out there on the open market, by the way – you just need to spend a bit of time scrolling and you WILL find them. I found a one bed flat valued around £65K, and had offered £35K for it. After a bit of back and forth on emails between the agent and myself, we ended up agreeing a £40K purchase price, but it wasn't one I wanted to buy for myself so I punted it to this guy I knew in London to say it was agreed and asked if he wanted to buy it. He transferred a £4K fee into my bank account, I sent a couple of emails to lawyers instructing them to engage and deal with this. I was basically just an agent in the middle for this one, but I made £4K for about 30 minutes work, from a beautiful beachside location, as I sipped on prosecco for my breakfast. The buyer was happy with the discounted property at such a low value and high yield. The seller was "content", I guess – maybe not "happy", considering he was selling for £25K (or 35%!) less than the value from the home report. The selling agent was happy, as we'd got one of his listings sold. And me? Well, I was fucking delighted! Really, this game need not be complicated.

Anyway, get a good team in place, send some emails, deal with a bit of admin, and you will be off to the races. You want to spend more time doing what you want to do and less time pissing about with stuff that other people can do on your behalf. These power team members will do it better than you ever will too. It's worth every single penny they charge, so you can continue to build your business in the background. Leverage other peoples' time to free up your own.

IT & Systems

I think it's probably fair to say that most folk probably don't value the importance of the IT side of business. Certainly, when it comes to systems and systemisation, please, please, please, if you think you do not value that, *please* go back and revisit that thought process! Systems should operate in the background with minimal involvement from your side, to still achieve awesome results with the minimum amount of time input. Keeping your files and folders organised is a big deal too – trust me. When it comes to year end and your accountants ask you for all the files such as invoices, bank statements, completion statements, lender statements, pictures, tenancies, deal analyses, and all the questions that go along with all of that, you do not want to be in a position where you simply say "eh!?" and you don't know where to start. It can either be a small repetitive daily task to keep on top of your files and folders, or it can be a monumental task at year end that will take up a shit tonne of your time when you didn't expect it, mixed in with mass confusion because you can't find half the stuff being requested. To be honest, even if you don't take this on board from reading it here from me now, it's highly likely that as you grow and get a bit more experience in all this type of stuff, you will value it and implement it from that point in time. It's definitely better to get into that habit now, though. It takes 28 days to create a new habit, apparently, so do it now and you will be forever grateful to yourself! Oh, and grateful to me too for telling you to be more organised.

It's 2025 – we're about to colonise Mars, apparently, so we can all make sure we're not operating at dinosaur IT levels with physical folders containing lots of pieces of paper. Right?! It's 2025 – we will all store our files in a cloud based storage platform such as OneDrive, Google Drive, iCloud, etc., etc. Assuming you do store your documents in the cloud, then every document from every deal, at any time, will be available to you on any device, whenever you need it, for whatever purpose, so you can keep deals moving along regardless of whatever you're up to, wherever you are in the globe.

You do not need a fancy website or domain or brand or font consistency when you're starting out your property business. You need a free email account from GMail or similar, so you can communicate, and you need a cloud based storage platform for your files and folders. As you grow, depending on your objectives for the business, you can consider getting a bit more professional on the branding front, but for right now you just want to focus on getting deals done. No power team member gives a shit about a fancy website or brand, so it doesn't make sense to spend your time and focus on that, certainly in the early days.

Time & Focus

I've mentioned all the crazy ideas we had when we were starting out, for the multiple businesses of all shapes and sizes that we started up, rather than just spending our time focused on the ONE thing that we wanted to go after. I guess at the start we didn't really know, hence us trying out various different things. Ultimately though, the more things you are focusing on, the more time depletion and lack of focus you will have on each one. More time and more focus on one thing will always serve you better than less time and less focus on multiple things. If you compare yourself to someone else who does nothing but focus on one of the things that you have in your arsenal of time suckers, they will, in most cases, smoke you.

I've come to get a lot more precious on my time since we started in business. It's funny to think about now, because in the beginning I would go out of my way to meet people, commit my time, help them, all for nothing. I really did want to help others succeed. Whilst that is still the case for me – in fact I'm very passionate about helping others, as we all are at Team REAL – it has to be on the basis of monetary exchange for our services. Bizarrely, I remember travelling up and down the country to meet people, spending time in these meetings with no purpose. Constantly meeting up with people simply to have a coffee so they could pick my brain! Absolutely mental. Nothing in it for me, but plenty in it for the one doing the brain picking! There are so many folk out there that think property is some kind of magic bullet – the "Willy Wonka Golden Ticket", as I like to refer to it at live events when talking about others' false perceptions of what it takes to achieve success in any business, property included. There are so many people that will suck the life out of you for nothing in return. So much time, effort and energy can be lost when you're not laser-focused and precious with your time. All the books written by entrepreneurs talk the same talk when it comes to time.

Even if I think about when I first started We Buy Homes Scotland, I was spending a lot of money on marketing – mainly on flyers and Google PPC at the time, spending a lot of time on calls with vendors, getting leads in across the country, travelling around a lot and putting in a shit tonne of time to get these deals ready to trade. I had decent deals! But I ended up buying most of them myself, because the pool of buyers I had were just unreliable. Everyone, and I mean EVERYONE, says they want to buy discounted property deals. The reality is that most of our clients, even now, wouldn't be in a position to get deals over the line without the framework of our support – there's so much work that goes on in the background that just isn't seen. It still fascinates me how people can expect to go on a three day course to learn about property sourcing – a professional skill that takes years to master – and come out with a wee certificate at the end saying they're now qualified to go and take on the existing market of established businesses who are dominating that space. Don't get me wrong, I'm a firm believer that anyone can do anything when they put their minds to it, but there is definitely a case of over-simplification out there in the "property training" space, where dreams are made out to be achievable just because you rocked up to a course to learn about the subject. I've been sold the dream before – and if it wasn't for Alex Robertson and Conar Tracey, who knows where I'd have ended up.

We insist to our clients that they focus on two things – raising money and buying deals. The rest of the strategy will take care of itself if process is followed. We have too many clients now achieving so many awesome results for there to be any doubt about our model. The ones that follow the process, continually raising money and buying deals... they are the ones who create the most success along the way.

Most folk tend to think about starting a property business to create an extra income and build wealth – both of which are very valid and attractive targets. But really, we want the income and we want the wealth, so we can have more freedom and more time. More income allows us to travel more, take more time off, spend more time doing the things we want and love to do, rather than just being "at work" 5 out of 7 days, or 70% of the time. So every time you do a property deal, and you're working towards creating an increased overall wealth position, it's really all about what you can do with that time you will create for yourself because of your increased earnings. I'm not even sure people actually care so much about the actual money itself – it seems to be the feeling of having the money that's more what we crave. Even using the money to buy things that you want to have, once you have them, it's the feeling of having them that seems to be what's desirable. I don't think it's any different with having more time. I think we would all want more time if we had the ability to create it, and that's really what we're doing when building a property business. Whilst it's not necessarily as passive as some of the gurus make out, there are a lot of things that can go on in the background through systemisation and your power team that frees up your time to do more of what you love to do. The real currency of this crazy thing called life, is time.

Leverage (Eliminate, Delegate, Outsource & Know Your Value)

There's an interesting principle about leverage that you may or may not have been exposed to previously. It's based around your calculated hourly rate, consequently what you should spend your time doing, then comparatively what others should do for you (assuming you can outsource, or leverage, other peoples' time at a cheaper rate than what it would cost you to do it, if you applied your own hourly rate to whatever task needed done). Example as follows...

If you earn £120K per year, based on working 20 days out of each month, that means you work 240 days of the year, earning £500 per day. Let's assume you work 9 hours per day, so your hourly rate would then be equated to £500 / 9 hours = an rate of £55.56 per hour. Obviously, being an entrepreneur, it's highly likely you will work more than 9 hours a day, and probably even more than 365 days per year too! But we'll work off the above calculations for the basis of the example...

The principle suggests that (in this example) all tasks which cost you less than £55.56 per hour should be outsourced to others. It makes sense, I guess, in theory anyway. Equally, I really don't mind cutting my grass. Or putting the bins out. Or cleaning the kitchen worktop if it's dirty. Or filling up the dishwasher. Or looking after my kids. Or putting a clothes washing on. Or doing a bit of DIY, whatever that may be. Or tidying up the endless mess that is the kids' toys scattered all over the house when they should be contained to the playroom! Now I must confess, I do like the finer things in life, so whilst I don't mind some of these tasks I do mind some of them, and we do have support from others to assist with some things around the house, and it does make a massive difference to our lives. I guess I value time exchange for some tasks more than others. But I'm just saying I'm not so precious about this principle of outsourcing absolutely everything to others – I like a bit of hard graft, and get a great sense of satisfaction by completing certain tasks.

When it comes to business, we are a bit more serious around this. When we got started up, for example, I did all the graphic design and media stuff, as I had a base knowledge from when I studied HND Multimedia Design & Production at Glasgow College of Building & Printing. (I think that place has been shut down now, actually, and it's a bit of an eyesore – you will notice it if you're ever driving into Glasgow city centre.) But there was no way in our early days we could've justified spending thousands with a freelancer or a media company to create some graphics or fliers or logos, etc. Now, we have a full-time marketing manager, in-house, and a media team of three (including a full-time videographer and social media manager). Things will change as you grow, as they did for us.

Then there's the management of all the rental properties – an administrative nightmare as you scale. Some people reading or listening to this book might think that managing your own properties is the way to go, to keep costs down and maximise cashflow. Well, whilst that may be true, if you are managing your own stock you will be tied up constantly dealing with tenants, maintenance issues, arrears, filling voids, and you will find that you struggle to get the TIME to FOCUS on what really matters as a professional property investor – and that's 1) RAISING MONEY and 2) BUYING DEALS! Leverage, in this case, is absolutely critical, in my view. There are so many different things that your letting agent will take care of on your behalf, all happening in the background, so you can sit on the beach sinking Piña Coladas like there is no tomorrow! I'm not sure about you, but I don't want to hear from tenants at all, never mind when I'm on the beach sinking Piña Coladas. It's really interesting to me that people have such different views on the letting agent thing. I know massively successful people that manage their own units – I personally just cannot understand why they don't outsource that area of their business. Letting agents typically charge around 10%+VAT for the management element of their business – that is worth every single penny, in my book (as you can see here, literally)! One aspect you do need to watch, though, are the costs they try to charge you for maintenance issues – things like lease finding or marketing fees, inventory check-in fees, inventory check-out fees, etc. This seems to be how these guys make their money. Make sure you keep an eye on this, as we've known multiple agents to try to take the piss with these sorts of things and that's where you will really bleed costs if you are not analysing the performance of your portfolio on a regular basis.

A summary of this section is a bit of "each to their own". Always remember that this business is YOUR business, so nobody (including me!) should be telling you what to do. You should take all the information given to you, from this book and other sources, which will allow you to take an informed decision as to what you feel is the best course of action to create the best result for you and your business. Ultimately, though, if you want to scale – and I assume you do, to some degree at least — unless you're one of these random folk that only want one property as a nest egg (whatever the fuck that means) – if you want to scale then you must leverage, so understand the principles and then decide how you want to use your precious time.

Branding & Credibility

We were guilty in our early days of this same thing, and I think everybody is. Everyone wants to create a brochure for their investors. Everyone wants a cool company name and a brand. Everyone wants to choose their colours and company logo and the font type, and to be involved in the overall design and give their tuppence-worth on the new website and choose the pictures and and and and and....! But really, all this stuff really doesn't matter when you're starting out. As I explained earlier in the book, really you just need a laptop, a mobile, an email account, a printer/copier/scanner, and a drive to succeed! Again, have a think about where you're spending your time and why. You are not a graphic designer. You are not an accountant. You are not a letting agent. You are a professional property investor, and you should focus your time on raising money and buying deals, as that's what's going to create success in your property business.

But like I say, everyone is guilty of this kind of stuff at the start. We were no different. I would say, though, depending on your goals and ambition, you might want to think about it more than others, relative to where you want to take your operations.

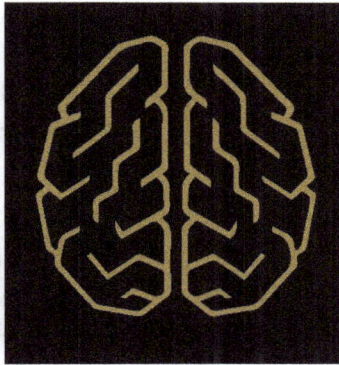

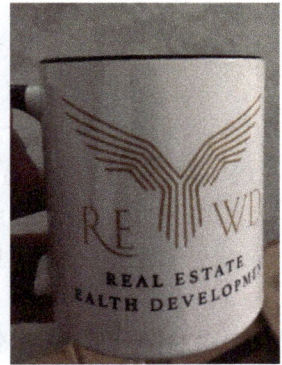

From the get-go, Alex and I always wanted to have a Group of companies, rather than just one single company. We set out to create a Group, with Group branding, individual company branding, synergistic tie-ins with the activities of each entity, etc., etc. So if you're thinking along the same lines, I'd counsel you to think more about branding. Our trademark logo is the black background with the gold wings – it's been with us from day one, in different guises, but I think is now relatively widely known for the association of REAL Property – I love that.

My totally super-awesome wife, Emma, has her own property investment company – Chlodan Properties – our kids names are Chloe and Daniel, hence the creative name of Chlo-Dan. She has no brand. She has no website. She has no social media presence (apart from when I post her deal examples). Literally the ONLY thing she has, that she's used to create a multimillion-pound property portfolio producing over £10K a month of gross rent in only two years since starting out in August 2023, using none of her own money, is a GMail email account – oh, and of course a printer/copier/scanner, for all those documents that go back and forth for acquisitions and refinances. It really does not need to be more complicated than that.

Now, this is probably an extreme too far for most, as assuming you want to attract external investment and demonstrate your credibility to the masses, as you grow you will want to create more awareness, then you will want to be more active on socials, and it's fair to think about branding at this point as you will want to stand out from the many one-man-bands out there talking the talk. In Emma's case, she is content kicking about in the background with this investment vehicle doing its thing, creating awesome results, and she doesn't want or need to be out there doing anything else. That might change in time, but for now it's ticking all the boxes and will continue to do so for the foreseeable.

One thing you must seriously consider as you scale, though, is the credibility of you and your business. What will people find when they look you up on socials, or dig into your company information on Companies House? By the way, if you've never been on Companies House, if this is new terminology to you, go on there and have a look around – it will open a whole other world to you. You can look into company details, their ownership, see Charges (i.e. who has funding secured against what assets), the Directors, other companies they are involved in, and most importantly their financial performance from their company accounts. Important to note that for most trading businesses you can only ever see their balance sheets, not their P&Ls, so you struggle to get a clear picture of exactly what they're up to. When it comes to property investment companies, however, you really can see what they're up to, and it's an easy way to assess who is truly active (i.e. who is walking the walk)! So, so many folk out there are operating on some mad kind of "fake it until you make it" type thing, doing all the talking the talk. This baffles me, as it's so easy to find out who the main players are. Have a look into some of our Group companies and see what you can find out:

- REAL Property Scotland Limited

- REWD Developments Limited

- REAL Estate Wealth Development Limited

- REAL ABR SPV 1 Limited

- REAL ABR SPV 2 Limited

So, for branding, I would say it depends on what stage you're at, but certainly in your humble beginnings it's not going to get you anywhere. Remember, I'm talking property investment business here rather than any other type of venture where branding might be essential from the word go. When it comes to credibility, though, every day you progress, you should be showing the world who you are, what you do, what you can do for others, and why you are a credible person with a credible business, that people should want to at least watch you and your progress and your journey. That's the funny thing about credibility – so many people will watch and watch and watch for ages and ages, before they engage with you and your offering, whatever that may be. But they definitely do watch, even if they don't engage. Socials are the best way to 1) instantly get your content out there into the hands of millions, and 2) build your following and credibility based on the content you're putting out there. If you've never done any social media stuff before or thought about building your own brand, whether that be corporate or personal or both, you might be quite surprised to see what comes out of a bit of regular posting! It still puzzles me to this day how crazy the social media thing is generally, but at the end of the day it's where most people nowadays spend most of their downtime, endlessly scrolling these social media channels, so it's where you will have the best chance to get noticed by many, if you do in fact put yourself out there to be seen. What can you do to stand out from the crowd and have the user stop scrolling down their feed? Time to get creative!

Scaling

As with any venture, it must start, get a grounding, prove the concept, and then it's time to scale it up. Not scaling is a very dangerous place to be, in my opinion. If I think back to the early days of REAL Property, where we only did £195K of revenue in 2021-2022, that scares the shit out of me! The year before was only £44K of revenue. Having these levels of turnover are surely unsustainable? I can't even remember what these revenues would've been back in the day. Now, though, we have multiple streams of revenue coming into that business, split up roughly into the following categories:

- Clients: education, mentorship, consultancy, events and ongoing support

- Off-market deal trading: sourcing BMV properties and selling to our clients

- Auction stock

- Refurbishments

- Estate Agency

Scaling comes with its PROs and CONs – obviously as you scale you have more staff, more expenses, and more overheads. There's just more of everything going on, and your business morphs from this small startup into a revenue-generating machine. I like to think about business as a machine. We're at a section of the book referring to systemisation, and if you get that right it can make a huge difference to the overall operation of your business.

I must confess, we are still constantly battling to refine our systems and processes. As I write this, I have taken a note to assess the direct debits of the business, as we are currently spending around £10K per month on all sorts of softwares, subscriptions, licences and various other "tech stuff". It's critical to review this on a six-monthly or annual basis, to ensure you aren't paying for things you don't use. Staff will sign up to subscriptions insisting that the latest app is required as it will allow us to do X with Y and generally make the business better.

The staff then move on, the business keeps paying for it, not even using the app anymore, but that direct debit just keeps rolling! The new guy comes in, they want their own spin on things, they get their new apps, increasing the overheads, but not cancelling down the old ones. Man, it's so easy for this stuff to creep up on you, and before you know it you're spending a fortune on shite that you don't even use!

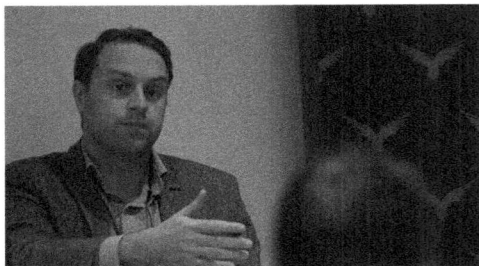

Anyway, we've scaled in a lot of different ways as we've grown. The portfolio has grown massively, and the types of opportunities we have now are just incredible. They are opportunities that we would never even have had a sniff of if we hadn't made all the other moves we did in the past. That's the one thing about the journey – as tough as it was, is, and will continue to be, the journey just wouldn't be the journey if it wasn't the journey. So many deals turned out to be completely different from how we thought they would pan out. So many problems have led us to a place of experience, wisdom and technical ability that so many others lack. Multiple staff members we've taken on have come and gone – there's staff we thought would be good that turned out not to be; so many folks seem to be very good at doing interviews but not so good at doing their jobs!

We get opportunities now, though, on a daily basis that most other people wouldn't even believe existed, on the portfolio side and the deals side generally. I've not even really talked about REWD Developments Limited (AKA 'DEV') throughout this book, albeit that I have mentioned it, but that business in itself ticks along in the background with minimal efforts and high profitability — it doesn't even have any staff or overheads as such, only direct costs associated with doing deals. That business will make around £500K per year profit in the 2025-2026 financial year, without us really doing much work. It's just another example of what I call "The Relentless Momentum Wave"! We've continued to scale, exponentially, across all areas of the Group, so now we have the ability to take on these types of deals, at scale, on the side. If you go to any of these "property education" events, and we really do not categorise ourselves as being in that space, you will hear all the gurus talk about "Multiple Streams of Income" — and that's what we have now in our scaled-up business, on steroids. What a beautiful machine.

DEV is a trading business focused on buying and selling properties, just to explain this model briefly, as it is highly profitable for minimal efforts. Maybe some folk reading this book would want to try it. Obviously if you think we can help you then feel free to reach out. Typically, we buy and put straight back into the auction for sale, without doing any work. For example, if the property is worth £100K and we secure it for £50K, then we put it into the auction and sell it for £80K, we've maybe made around £25K pre-tax profit within 1-2 months, and the buyer is delighted because they've purchased a property at 20% discount from its value. As we have always and continue to maintain, you will make your money when you buy — if you buy right, however you exit that deal, you will make money, somehow! That's the glorious thing about the off-market deal machine — and I mean the collective Group operations generally, not Mr Conar Tracey! (Although he is a glorious machine in his own right...) The off-market machine allows us to feed clients, ourselves to hold, ourselves to refurb to sell, or ourselves to flip straight back into auction and make a quick buck. From DEV's perspective, it only buys to sell into auction, or buys to refurb and sell on the open market – the latter is a bit more of a ball-ache, as there's a lot more time involved, a lot more capital deployed, and a lot more hoping and praying that the apparent buyer actually does conclude on the thing. That being said, a buy to refurb to sell can make a bit more profit in terms of value, but margins due to quicker timescales to profitability can be relative doing the straight auction flip model.

The point of highlighting all of these things to you here is to get the point across that all of this widespread opportunity has come with scaling. The daily single unit opportunities, the larger portfolios, the bigger discounts, the high ticket clients, the magnitude of deals per week, the fancy Glasgow city centre office, the social media presence, the position of the brand, the funding solutions, the efficiencies of refurbishments, the DEV activity, the credibility of us as individuals as well as the credibility of the REAL brand generally...

Ride the relentless momentum wave, enjoy every second of it, and just keep moving forward. For me, it's all about the journey rather than the destination. We have such good fun doing what we do – it's crazy to think about what life would be like if we never started down this path.

DEALS

Marketing

I remember growing up, through school, into my early adult years and to be honest even until a couple of years ago, I really did not understand marketing and I certainly didn't value it. It is absolutely incredible now, how much of a shift I've had in my respect for this area of business. In my corporate life, I never even had to think about marketing. It just wasn't even part of the business – it was such a different model. I was never exposed to it, I never had any experience in it, and I honestly saw the subject of marketing generally as some shitty job that involved newspapers, magazines, pictures, stories, billboards and lots of bollocks that I thought was uninteresting and had no place in my life! Like many views along my journey, how wrong could I be...?

Marketing now is at the forefront of our business. We spend around £50K per month at the moment across different areas of the Group, and every single day it's the ONE thing that goes back and forward in the REAL WhatsApp chats, with videos of different people explaining different strategies, that we try to understand and implement across our operations. It is fundamental to our business. Without marketing, nobody would know us, we would get no enquiries / no leads, we would have stagnated and would not have scaled.

It's so funny for me to think back to the very first moves I ever made when starting out. It was all marketing for We Buy Homes Scotland. I had leaflets being distributed door to door, I had billboards at the side of the road, I had a guy walk about Falkirk High Street with a sandwich board, I was on the TV, I was in toilets at service stations, I was on the radio, I had business cards left in local boozer toilets, I had bandit boards up all over town, I was on buses, I was doing Facebook adverts, I was doing Google PPC (that's pay per click) – you name it, We Buy Homes Scotland was out there, everywhere, for everyone to see. But I did not have a scooby fucking doo what I was doing! Whilst I chucked everything and the kitchen sink at the marketing side as I tried to get this new homebuyer brand off the ground, I was throwing money down the drain. I never had any means to generate revenue. Even if I did get a deal signed up, and admittedly there were a few, I would buy the property myself rather than trade it on, and consequently generate zero revenue. I wasn't even thinking about this venture as a business. I was just a guy with a dream that saw an opportunity and I wanted to give it a right good go. What was the alternative? Stay stuck in a job I hated for the rest of my days? No way – I had to at least try. Even then, I had no respect for marketing. The total loss to Emandel Property Trading Limited, as it was known back in the day, was around £100K. ONE HUNDRED THOUSAND POUNDS OF LOSSES. Unbelievable. That said, we wouldn't be doing what we are now if it wasn't for that experience back then, so I don't regret it, but as that old saying goes, "if I only knew back then what I know now...!"

Fast-forward to 2025 now as I write this book, and what a journey the marketing side of our business has been on. We now have a dedicated in-house marketing manager, Leigh, who controls all marketing across the Group, focusing on digital marketing, although we do have some other more traditional methods in play such as flier distribution, and I include social media within that too. Marketing is the lifeblood of our business – it is a constant revolving plate of opportunity, bringing in leads for new clients and new vendors, as well as creating a much wider and aggressive exposure for our corporate and personal brands.

We have a lot of deal–hungry clients, so we keep this tap turned on at all times, to ensure they remain fed. If you want to do deals, you first need the leads. Once you have the leads, it's a whole other story about converting them to generate revenue. It's also a whole other story ensuring that the buyer and vendor remain focused on getting the deal over the line – so many people do not appreciate what's involved. I certainly never did when I was getting started.

You might be thinking about doing your own marketing to generate your own leads to build your own business. That's where I started out in terms of thought process. I must say though, honestly, I feel so lucky to have gotten out of that mess of the £100K loss. I wish someone had said the same to me as I'm about to say to you now – just pay someone else a sourcing fee, factor the costs into the deal, and assuming you want to build up your buy to let portfolio, just keep raising money buying deals, and you will get to where you want to be. You will use your money so much more effectively that way, as long as you "buy right", of course. I appreciate there will be people out there that want to start a sourcing business and don't want to build up a portfolio – for those of you in this category, well, you really don't have much of a choice: you must use marketing, whatever the guise, to generate leads for you to convert to revenue. "Sourcing" is a trading business – you will need to start thinking about systems, processes, staff and overheads as you scale things up. Just please remember that when you get a lead, it's highly likely we've also got that same lead, and we have a powerful machine behind us to get that deal done. I'm a firm believer in that anyone can achieve anything, and I LOVE to see people succeed, but in that environment when it's We Buy Homes Scotland versus a new one-man-band sourcer guy, the likelihood is that we will smoke you, every time!

Sourcers

Leading on from the previous section, it's really important to understand the sourcing market generally. Who are the main players, who are the wannabes, who does all the talking but none of the walking (and there's plenty of the latter!)? Unfortunately, there's a lot of these "property training" courses running up and down the country where you can learn how to be a sourcer and, after attending a four-day course, be ready to compete with professionals that have been in the game for years already, immediately quit your job, be your own boss, make £10K per deal traded, trade five deals a month, and then that's you sorted for life! But of course, in the REAL world, that's not how it goes. What these courses do create, though, is a flood to the housing market of unprofessional, unqualified, inexperienced "property sourcers", trying to flog all the shite of the day, often with no control whatsoever over the vendor and the situation. Many of the deals don't even make sense from an investment perspective. We've heard so many horror stories of fees being paid to these types of people, with no cigar provided at the end. No credit provided, no other deal, no refund, no support, no alternative solutions, just money paid from an unsuspecting investor to a wannabe, then the wannabe disappears. Scary place to be.

Obviously social media is a great place to start when you're looking to suss out who you should do business with – just don't believe everything you see or hear on socials! Plenty of folk are good storytellers, but after a bit of digging you can quickly find that they lack substance. Companies House is always a good place to go looking for more in-depth analysis of someone you're looking to build a relationship with. There can be pros and cons to one-man-bands versus professional sourcing companies, but ultimately, if you are educated well enough to spot the good from the bad, both in terms of your potential suppliers as well as the investment opportunities themselves, you will be in the best placed position to make informed decisions. Many of these unprofessional outfits, regardless of the size of their operation, will put deals out available for sale, without showing the total investment value required, which in turn provides an inaccurate representation of the returns. For example, many people do not factor in their sourcing fees into the deal analysis, because if they did, they know the deal would look nowhere near good enough for someone to want to buy it. So, they hide it, to make the deals look better than they actually are.

I had a meeting a couple of months back with a new client – they came into the office and sat down to discuss onboarding with us, and told me about the recent deal they had bought from what I would call a "dodgy sourcer". One of those types of sourcers that hide fees, and who in this case had very suspicious general Terms of Business, making deals look way better than they are, and were known to more experienced investors to have a lack of credibility in the market...

There was a £7K+VAT fee to be paid up front, without a deal even being there in the first place. This fee then allowed the "sourcer" to go and start looking for a deal. Once the sourcer had found a deal, it would be presented to the client. If the sourcer presented three deals to the client and the client said no every time (even if the deals were completely shit!), the fee was then claimed by the sourcer, and no further deals would be presented! The Terms were made clear to the client before engagement, the client accepted the said Terms, and the sourcer then began to work on creating a solution. It may or may not surprise you to hear that this is not the first time we've heard this, either – so many clients that come to work with us, for whatever reason, have started out this way, only realising their mistake a bit further down the line, once they've become a bit more experienced.

So a deal was presented, at a £52K purchase price. End value expected at £65K. On the face of it, could it be OK? Well, maybe, but let's analyse... No home report since off-market. Applicable ADS at the time was 6%. Refurb was budgeted at £10K ex VAT. Cash purchase was stated to be necessary for rapid completion (i.e. within 8 weeks – that's right, *8 weeks*). Legal fees on top call it £1.5K. I'm not sure if you can see how many things are wrong with this, so I'm going to break it down into a line-by-line analysis below, before we discuss it further:

Purchase price   £52K

ADS at 6%   £52K * 6% = £3,120

Refurb   £10K+VAT = £10K or £12K (noting VAT may or may not be applicable depending on the contractor(s) used, so we'll be generous here and assume no VAT)

Finance costs   £0 (since cash conclusion suggested to allow 'quick' completion)

Legals   £1.5K

TOTAL COSTS   £52K+£3,120+£10K+£1.5K = <u>£66,620</u>

So bearing in mind the end value of this deal is expected to be £65K, if we refinanced this at 75% of this value we would obtain a mortgage at £48,750, meaning we have left around £18K in this deal. Or have we...? Who forgot about the £7K+VAT up-front sourcing fee?! £7K+VAT = £8.4K, and we'll assume the fee isn't paid through a VAT registered business so it is not recoverable. So that's another 8 thousand 4 hundred pounds to be added into the total costs of the deal here. Cash required for this one deal then moves from £67K odds up to £75K. SEVENTY-FIVE THOUSAND POUNDS invested into this ONE deal!? Guys – please – for the love of god – make sure you understand these basic calculations before you go out there and start buying properties from people you don't know. This type of stuff scares the shit out of me. We want to see people succeed and grow successful businesses – this type of deal does nothing but pull you right back down, and damages your chances of creating any kind of success at all. Cash left in, factoring in ALL costs into this deal, whether shown in the deal presentation or not, then becomes £26.5K. You'd be lucky to generate say £300 per month cashflow before voids, arrears and maintenance on this deal, so it would take you around 88 months operating at full occupancy with no other costs to recoup that cash. Genuinely un-believable. And I know there's not a dash in the word "unbelievable", but I write it with a dash to create a short gap when I say it (or you read it) to overemphasise just how crazy this situation is. Worst part is, this is just one deal example from one dodgy sourcer – this stuff goes on every day, and all over the UK. There are plenty of sourcers making decent money from these types of deals too, and there are of plenty inexperienced buyers buying them!

Eight weeks, by the way, is not a quick completion. You can conclude with bridging in under four weeks if you have a decent supportive funder and a good legal team. There is no need to tie up that amount of cash in one single deal for a completion that allows eight weeks. If something needs to be done in three weeks, then fine – to guarantee the deal, maybe cash would be required then, but even if it was, you could still bridge short-term if you wanted or needed to, after the purchase but before you refinanced it on to a long-term fund. Another example of more wool being pulled over inexperienced eyes. I imagine the only reason this sourcer has suggested cash is more to protect themselves from any backlash of the deal potentially falling apart since they likely had no control over the vendor in the first place.

Anyway, I hope that's hit home. But let's think about an alternative option for my poor client here, who has, simply put, been sold a dream and then been shafted. Remember that deal was off-market, so there was no HR, no survey, no condition report. Simply a few pictures to decide on. Now that's fine by the way, when we're talking off-market, heavily discounted deals – that's part of the game. You won't always get a survey in off-market deals, and in fact in most cases you won't, nor will you even get to view. But when it comes to deals that require this amount of cash to buy and leave this amount of cash in at refi, surely it would make more sense to buy something at full market value, with a survey, after a viewing, to minimise your risk, if this level of cash was what you were content to sacrifice into one unit? I'm not suggesting for a second that makes investment sense, by the way; I'm just saying if that was to be your view, for whatever reason, then it does not make sense to me to factor in all the risk of an off-market deal when you could buy something from the open market, using this case as an example:

So if we bought on the open market for £65K, assuming walk-in condition, then ADS would still apply, no refurb though, plus legals, means all in the cash would be:

Purchase price	£65K
ADS at 6%	£65K * 6% = £3.9K
Refurb	£0
Finance costs	£0 (we'll continue to assume cash is necessary to allow this supposed "quick" completion of 8 weeks)
Legals	£1.5K
TOTAL COSTS	£65K+£3.9K+£1.5K = £70.4K (versus the 75K cash required for the off-market option)

That deal was not a deal. It doesn't make financial sense. Yet our new client bought it because they didn't understand. They didn't know any different, until they came in to speak to us to get a different perspective on how this game is played professionally.

In REAL Property Scotland, we have deal calculators that allow you to simply type in these details and it will analyse deals automatically for you. For anyone interested in this, just get in touch with me and we can send ours over for you. Even with the automatic calculators though, it's still best to work through the numbers manually in my opinion, as it helps you to understand the way the numbers flow.

Anyway, we're talking about sourcers here, and I just wanted to get the point across that it's often the case that things are not as they seem. Stay vigilant, do your due diligence, make sure you understand the numbers, then – if you're content with the information and you think it makes investment sense – pull the trigger and get the deal done. Obviously, for anyone that wants any support on this type of stuff, that's exactly what we offer, so just reach out and let us know where you think we can help you grow.

On Market

Deals can definitely be found on the open market. Note that sourcers will trade deals both on and off-market, and just because a sourcer has brought you a deal that is on-market doesn't mean you shouldn't pay them for their services, or turn your nose up at it. If you were to go and cut them out, which short-sighted people do now and again, you certainly won't get any more deals from that supplier, and you'll also be well known to the market, very quickly, as someone who sourcers should not do business with. You can find your own deals on the market too! We are testament to that. I'll give you some examples of on-market deals we've done in a minute. If it's a deal, it's a deal, so pay the fee (if you've not found the deal yourself) and buy it. One thing is for sure, the more deals you buy, the quicker you pay, the better you are to deal with as a client, the more deals will come your way. People do business with people, and as with any business relationships are key to both your and your suppliers' successes. As always, make sure you've done your due diligence, and you're comfortable with the deal and all the details, before pushing the purchase button.

Home reports, in Scotland, are required for selling properties on the open market. So if there's an opportunity that is on the market, it should have a home report and it should be up to date (i.e. within the last 12 weeks), to allow you to analyse the details of that survey. Home reports contain information on the property condition, a financial valuation provided by the surveyor, as well as things like size, construction type, the energy performance certificate, and any suggested scopes of work that could improve that efficiency, insurance reinstatement value, as well as a property questionnaire that should be completed by the seller.

If you have this detail AND you can still get a juicy discount on the property, then it's a beautiful place to be.

A few of our deals have been secured on the open market from simply putting the time in to browse around and make offers. Yes, they are "cheeky" offers – of course they are – but I don't know the people I'm buying from, I will never meet them, there is no relationship there. I am just a guy with a goal that is unemotionally attached to proposals made. The vendor is the one who has the decision to make on whether or not they will accept the proposal and / or be offended by it! You really have to be OK with rejection – it's never been a problem for me! We cannot control other peoples' reactions; we can only try to control our own, so I don't think twice about making an offer that I know can work for us. People can be offended. Some people simply say "no thank you". Others reply with a "you are crazy to think I would sell at this price!" kind of line, and that can be a response even if the property has been on the market for over a year with little to no interest. It fascinates me. The home report system in Scotland can cause this type of false expectation for vendors – they can look at the home report valuation ONLY and don't consider any variations to market conditions or situations, and in the most part homeowners don't have the same specialist knowledge and expertise as we do as professional property investors, so they don't appreciate any comments when we try to justify our positioning of proposed purchase price. Sometimes if a vendor has too high a debt value, this can restrict their minimum sale price, so deals can sometimes be non-starters because of this, unless the seller will put cash into the deal themselves just to get rid of their existing security. It's always good to understand the debt value of a vendor, as you can use this to your advantage, since it will improve your negotiating position.

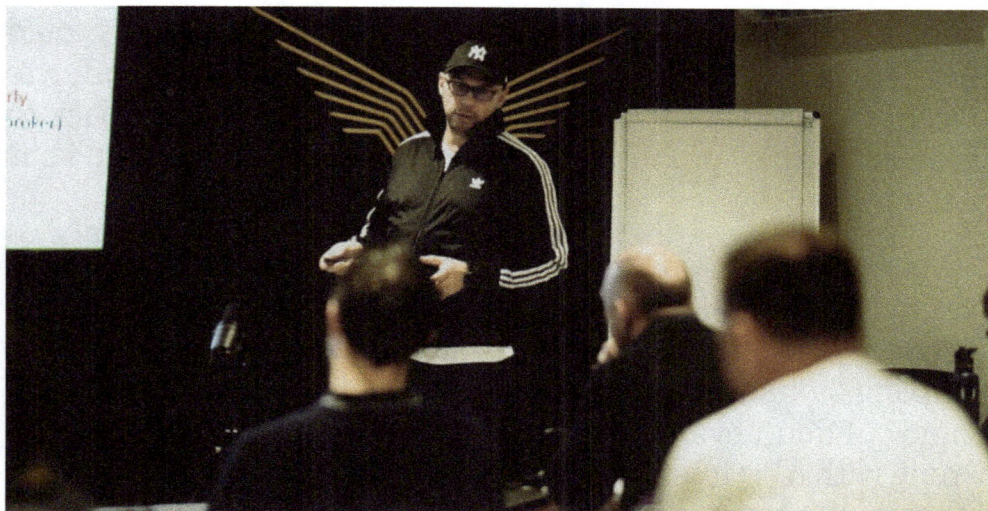

Now and again though, a belter comes along...

One of the first ever deals I bought was in a place called Kirriemuir, close to Dundee, in Scotland. It was on the open market and valued at £90K. It had been on the market for a while, I think about six months, and hadn't had much interest. From a homeowner's perspective, it's not the type of property many folk would want to buy to live in. For the rental market though, it would rent all day long, but the current owners had no intention of renting – they just wanted to get rid of it and move on with their lives. I, cheekily, sent an offer to the sellers for 40K (which is just below the ADS threshold, for anyone not aware). Deals getting done under 40K means no tax to pay. We investors love it because we like saving on tax – but not only that, we can also use the ADS as a negotiating tool in situations like this, since extra costs can make deals not stack, so it's max 40K purchase price or we're out. Now, even if we're not out at max 40K, we can still say that, judge the responses, then decide on whether or not we want to increase our offering. Even if we do increase our proposed purchase price, that could come with additional caveats

81

such as furniture included, involve funding (ie. the process could take longer), or various 'subject to' clauses within the offer to purchase. All these things might still push the vendor back to taking the initial proposal, so they're good ideas to keep in your arsenal.

Anyway, I offered £40K, and they said "no way"! But they countered at £45K. At this point, it was very early on in my journey, and of course I immediately started to shit myself, thinking "what have I missed, what's going on here, what do I do now, I don't even have the money, there must be something wrong with it", etc. etc. etc! Funnily enough, because of that fear, I then took a hard stance and said something like "sorry, this is my max price as it has to make investment sense for me". This was all going back and forth on emails by the way – within about 5-10 minutes of my initial price proposal. So it was all moving really fast and I was, in all honestly, pretty scared but excited at the same time. They came back again shortly after and said "Okay, we will accept your offer of £40K if you can conclude in three weeks from today." I was totally gobsmacked. This shit really works. I hadn't even done anything, really! Okay, apart from a couple of emails back and forth. So this was now my first even open-market deal that was, on the face of it, a proper belter! I went to view it the next day; it was actually a nice little pad, no issues for me, so I got the offer in on basis of a cash purchase to conclude in three weeks. Next issue, I had to find the money to buy it...

Richard Branson once said: "If someone offers you a great opportunity, say 'yes', then figure out how you're going to make it happen."

I had a home report of this property at £90K. There was nothing untoward. I had agreed a purchase price at £40K. That's over 50% of a discount against valuation. "I had to make money out of this, somehow!"

I approach a few folk who I knew had some cash in the bank, and seemed to (very easily) get the funds I needed on the basis of a 10% APR return, unsecured, paying out pro-rata for however many months I actually ended up using the money for. I then cracked on with the purchase, got the deal over the line in the three weeks, tarted it up a bit for a few grand, stuck it on the market for rent at £550 per month, and had a tenant in there after a month of concluding on the purchase. At the time, I had to wait six months before I could start the refinance process – we don't need to wait this long any more FYI, with multiple lenders offering the 'day 1 refi' option – so I put the application in, got the surveyor out, he valued it at £90K, the bank lent me 75% of that, and so I received £67.5K of cash back into my bank account. I repaid the investor back around £45K and I had created

a tax free cash position in my business of £25K odds. Unbelievable.

I. COULD. NOT. BELIEVE. WHAT. THE. FUCK. JUST. HAPPENED...!

I'd made my moves, I'd tested the model, and now I finally had a result that proves it all works. Jackpot!

This was to be the first of many belter deals we would do in our time. Now, we live and breathe this type of stuff every day. And OK, it's not every day a deal like this one comes along, but they *are* out there, and they are on the open market too. Only taking action will prove this to you, if you are struggling to grasp it.

Various other deals were done around this same time, buying three units for £50K each, all with £65K vals, all from open market. One at £40K valued at £65K. I did one more recently for Emma's Chlodan where we purchased a three-bed townhouse for £61K, valued at £100K. These were all on the open market. No marketing spend. Nothing fancy. Just a bit of self-belief, a bit of balls, a bit of pressure, a few cheeky offers, and sensational results. At this stage in our journey, with the knowledge and experience we have in this game, we know it better than anyone, inside out, and now regularly provide on and off-market investment opportunities to our clients, to allow them to grow their own businesses the way we have ours. It's funny to think back about all these deals, back in the day, when I was just a young man with a dream of creating some kind of massive success. Let my progress be a demonstration to anyone – you can achieve whatever you want in life, *IF* you are prepared to go out and make it happen.

Off-Market

So the deals are out there – yes, on the open market too! Maybe you believe me now after a few of these examples mentioned above? But in all honesty, the REAL deals come from the off-market space – there is nothing quite like getting "direct to vendor". And some of the deals we've done off-market are even better than the ones we've done on-market. The thing with off-market trading is to recognise that we are creating a solution for people in need. Often we hear about the "three Ds" – death, debt and divorce. 99% of the time, there are no issues with the property – the reason these people are willing to sell their properties at a reduced price compared to what the might obtain on the open market is due to their circumstances, not necessarily something to do with the integrity of the property.

Home reports are not required when buying or trading off-market deals, so yes, there is a degree of risk that comes with this. But when you're buying a property for 30% below what it's worth, you're expecting there to be some kind of trade-off for that! Well, you should be, but unfortunately some people still expect mint condition properties, no risk, everything to be 100% accurate and perfect, even in the wide and varied stressed scenarios of the vendors – they tend to be the types of clients that don't last too long. I've said it before and I'll say it again: those who study mindset and work on improving their overall mind control and subsequent actions and reactions are the ones who continually outperform those who don't. Getting better at dealing with problems is what's going to allow you to massively succeed. Like any venture, any growth, any challenge, there's going to be problems every step of the way. Remember, you are an entrepreneur – and yes, like it or not, if you start a business, you are an entrepreneur to some degree! An entrepreneur's job is to continually solve problems and create successes when it might seem like there are none.

From our perspective of being a professional sourcing business, we always ensure we tick a few essential pieces of criteria for our clients:

- We, or one of our trusted partner agents, have visited the property to assess the overall condition

- We have taken a selection of pictures as a minimum, if not also a video walkthrough

- We have assessed the refurbishment costs on the basis of the available exit solutions (as appropriate to the deal), including compliance costs, if any

- We have the seller (and consequently, the deal) secured through tight legal contracts

- We protect our clients (the buyers) from the sellers trying to sell to anyone else, including financial penalties for any breach

- We have put forward attractive financial terms from our finance partners for acquisition (bridging) funding

- We have assessed what makes sense in terms of exit solution and given our opinions / experience on what should work and why

- We have provided the basics of the property information such as:

  - Full address including postcode

  - The size in sqm

- The EPC rating, if available

- The number of bedrooms

- The type of property (house, flat, terraced, semi etc.)

- The expected end value of the property

- The expected funders available at exit and their terms (LTV, rates and fees), as applicable

- The cashflow analysis (both on acquisition, as well as exit), whatever exit option you choose, including information on exiting the deal as a:

  - Serviced Accommodation (average nightly rate, occupancy level and associated operational costs)

  - Standard BTL on the open rental market (professional workers, DSS tenants, retired tenants, etc.)

  - Mears Rental (government appointed body to house asylum seekers)

  - Flip (expected sales value, sales costs, expected timelines, projected profitability)

- The expectation of what amount of cash will be left locked in (or extracted from!) the deal at refi, if holding

- The total cash required to do the deal, whether purchasing cash or with other leveraged funding (recognising importantly here that this includes ALL costs – no hidden fees!)

- ○ The number of months until an "infinite return" is created, as applicable

If you follow multiple people online who claim to be a sourcer, you will find that they rarely talk, if at all, about all these types of things that are absolutely fundamental to analysing any opportunity correctly. The basics might get posted into a chat group or an email mailing list or a Facebook "deals" group, but 99% of the time they are lacking critical details, and even when specific details are requested you might find you are shot down for even asking the question. It's bizarre the way some people operate, and even more bizarre that folk buy deals from this type of "sourcer". We present deals to our clients with all the details and the full analysis to ensure complete transparency, which is in our clients' best interests as well as ours. Again, this comes down to firstly being in control of the deal, then having all the critical details, then understanding what in fact makes a good deal, then having the ability to get both buyer and seller on board to take the deal all the way to completion. The last part is an art in itself, never mind the rest of the process!

A couple of the deals we secured right at the start of our journey came through fliers posted through letterboxes of my local area in Falkirk. These two deals I'm about to explain were actually the two deals that got Alex and me into business together. I think Conar Tracey was just a sparkle in our eyes at this stage! I remember driving through to a viewing with Alex, telling him about these two deals I'd secured, but explaining that this sourcing business was going nowhere because I never had anyone to sell them to, and even if I did, I wouldn't want to, because the deals were so good I would want to keep them for myself! But the sourcing business (that is now REAL Property Scotland, by the way) needed revenue and cashflow, and it had neither! The cash balances were depleting month after month with all this marketing spend, with literally zero cash coming back in. We were discussing this generally, and we spoke about the idea for us to buy these deals together, but my sourcing business would get paid the sourcing fees which would allow us to continue to build the portfolio together, with some decent refinance opportunities, and I could then spend more on marketing to allow more deals to come in, to repeat the process and continue to grow together. This seemed like a no-brainer to me! I also loved how switched-on Alex was – he's just a really bright, well-educated, intelligent guy, and it gave me comfort by starting to work more with him. He's also always dealt with all the money and cashflow side of everything we've done, and he thinks about it on a level I still struggle to grasp! All that international finance exposure in his younger days has obviously served him (and consequently Conar and I!) very well.

When I explain the numbers of these deals in a second, I think it's fair to expect most folk will think I was absolutely mental to have "shared" these opportunities with anyone, rather than keep them for myself. And it is true, if I had done that, I could've made

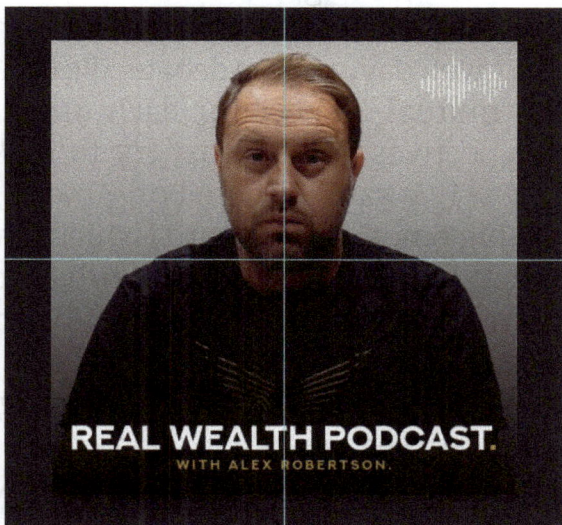

a shit tonne of money from them, continued to buy more deals, and grown my own portfolio. I do think that's short-sighted though, and it's certainly small-time thinking. I always wanted to have a BIG company, a serious one, a main player, and a Group of companies at that. Having a buy to let company on my own, with all the "passive income" coming in through rent, could've been good, but it would not have catapulted us into the business and growth that we have going on now. There's a saying that says, "if you want to go fast, go alone, but if you want to go far, go together." I absolutely fucking LOVE that.

"The team was greater than the sum of its parts", to quote one of our early statements from the website, explaining who we were and what we were doing. It's actually quite strange for me to think about how many people that start up in business and end up going through these mental disagreements and separations and newcos. I really do not feel that with Alex and Conar. We tend to have such varied yet balanced views, and I think it works so well because ultimately we are aligned on our objectives for moving the Group forward. We constantly discuss new ideas, changes to the model, pivoting, what deals we should focus on and why, staff base, and whatever else comes to mind any given day, and we debate. We don't always agree, but all have the mutual respect for each other to appreciate the others' perspectives and at least try to make sense of the alternative views. I've said to them both, many times – and obviously I'm the big emotional bastard (which is why I'm the one saying it!) – that I really love working with them, and I do hope that never changes. Accepting and respecting that business is complex to a degree that most will never understand. I do feel we've been really lucky in what we have going on, to have found a very balanced, yet aggressive approach to growth and success. All this has come from that point in time when I could've very easily

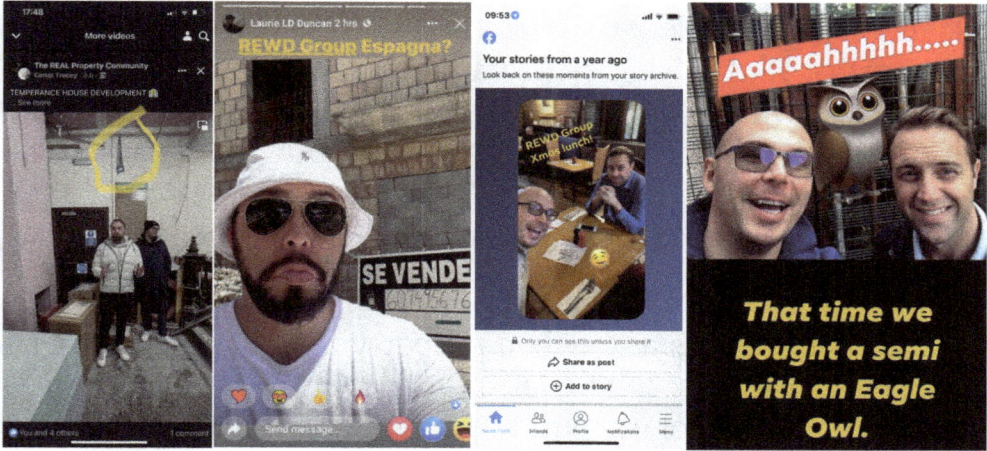

That time we bought a semi with an Eagle Owl.

cracked on, on my own, thinking only about myself. I choose the team, it kicked us into gear, and man oh man – I would not change that for the world!

Anyway, I digress slightly. So let's get back to the off-market deals that changed our overall direction of business...

It was back when I was trying to start my own sourcing business, not understanding what was truly involved to make a success of it, but having a go regardless to see what I could do. For anyone running or thinking of running a sourcing business, if you think about all the different ways to generate leads – and there's way more than you might think – distributing flyers is one that might get overlooked. Printed media versus digital media. A door canvasser walking about with a bag full of paper and posting leaflets through every letterbox in a block of flats, walking for miles per day simply posting flyers through door after door after door. Well, it might seem a bit old school, and it is, but if you think about the psychology of a vendor that receives a leaflet, and gets in touch with you from that leaflet to enquire about selling – that, my friends, is what you call a HOT LEAD! Why would someone go out of their way to call you after receiving a leaflet if they were not motivated to sell in some way? We didn't even realise all this back in the day – I was just having a go at it, with no knowledge or experience in all the marketing side like we do now. Both of these deals came from this exact same situation – the vendor received a leaflet through the door, called me, I went to view, got them signed up, then decided on how I could sell them out to make some money.

The first one was a two-bed property in Grangemouth. One of the mankiest places I've ever stepped foot in, in my whole life, ever, in the history of mankind. The vendor really was not living in good circumstances. He wanted to sell up, leave the house behind, go and get a camper van, and travel around Europe. The debt was around £20K on the property. I thought at the time it might have been worth around £70K, considering the condition it was in, but with a refurb it should've valued at well over 100K. I agreed with the vendor a sale price of £40K (just below the ADS threshold!), we could conclude in three weeks, he could move on and get his camper van, and we would have another property to add to the portfolio. So, to secure a two-bed semi for only £40K was an absolute belter of a deal. I could've bought it myself, but the sourcing business would have, yet again, generated no revenue. So, Alex and I agreed to buy it into our JV company, paying a £10K-odds sourcing fee to my sourcing business. We funded the acquisition with private investor cash, giving a 1st Charge Security against the property. We covered the seller's legal fees, he would release around £20K of cash from the sale, and everyone was happy. This refurb should've cost somewhere around £20K as a maximum, but it ended up costing us £35K in the end. This was at a stage in our journey where we didn't have a good team in place, and actually just relied on our letting agent's handymen team to go in and do the work, taking as long as it took, and paying a daily rate for however long that might have been. We can say it was a learning experience, for a LOT of different reasons. But anyway, we bought it, we refurbed it (using a secondary investor, with a 2nd Charge Security, for another £30K odds of cash), we tenanted it for around £650 per month, we refinanced it, and at the point of refinance, it was valued at £115K. We refinanced at 75% of the £115K, meaning we had a new loan of £86K from the term loan funder. £86K minus the first investor of £40K, minus the second investor of £30K, minus other fees and costs, etc., meant we had basically created an all money out deal, cashflowing around £300 per month (pre-VAM), with an equity position of around £28K (that's the £115K minus the £86K term loan). Nice deal!

The second deal was a three-bed flat. Condition wasn't so bad here, but it was a bit dated and needed a light tart-up. I actually got the lead initially around twelve months before they called me back to ask to go and see them again. Twelve whole months – they always seem to come back around. The vendor asked if I could go back to meet with them at the property to discuss moving forward, as they had now found a new place to stay – I think it was a retirement home of some kind, and not too far from where they were staying now. They wanted it done quick, of course! And on this occasion, they wanted a hand in moving their furniture from this existing flat to their new home. Well, we like to go above and beyond, so I organised this with the guys doing the refurb, and the seller was delighted with that level of service. We actually concluded on this one in 10 days from agreeing the sale. It was a great deal. What made it more interesting though, was the fact that the seller asked me if I could do their price expectation of £22K. These flats were worth around £70K at that time. In negotiations, you never want to be first to make an offer. They asked me what price I could do, I asked them what price they needed, they asked if I could do £22K, I said yes, we signed the paperwork, was in legals that afternoon, then 10 days later – with the assistance of the handymen to move the furniture – they had their money in the bank and were in their new home! Absolute gold.

At this kind of price level there was no funding involved – I think we actually used credit cards for the cash to buy this one. Usual gameplan – got in, quick light refurb, including a kitchen wrap in this one (where you cover the old existing kitchen in a kind of vinyl wrap to make it look more modern), mainly painting & carpets, stuck on the rental market, and had it rented out within a week at £650 per month. Refinanced it around eight months later, got £70K on the val, and I'm sure by this point in the book I don't need to explain that was some tasty tax-free cash extracted from that deal. So these two deals really opened our eyes and made us start to think very differently about this other world that might exist out there. If we just kept repeating this process, adding deal after deal after deal to the portfolio, raising money from private investors, using creative finance strategies and combining those with creative acquisition strategies, we were going to have a monster of a buy to let property portfolio in a very short period of time.

Auction Houses

I never quite understood this until we got into business with Conar, who has always worked in auctions and off-market deal trading. I got it in principle, but didn't understand the intricacies the way I do now. Obviously we have our own auction house, and we're constantly developing that, so – being in the business ourselves now – we know perfectly how it all works. And if you take the time to think about it, it should make a lot of sense to you here as well. Auction houses list properties for sale that have seller circumstances around why they do not want to (or simply can't) put the property on the open market for sale. It's not really any different from selling off-market, apart from the terms around the sale (that's under Auction Conditions), the fact it will be listed openly for the market to see, and will likely achieve a sale price somewhere in between the on-market sale price and the off-market sale price. It's quite common for us, though, if properties are not selling on the auction, for the seller to reduce their price point over a period of time, which could make it become a decent investment opportunity that could then be sold off-market to one of our clients.

Then you think about the auction owners – the people generating all the leads and speaking to all these vendors. In this case, think about REAL Property receiving enquiries from people looking to sell their homes quickly. If someone wants to sell their property for £10K and we think it would sell in auction for £50K, then we would obviously buy that ourselves and then put it into the auction for sale, so we could make a profit simply from the willingness of the vendor to just have it disposed of quickly so they can move on. Even if it only sold for £25K, you get the gist that there can be some decent profit in there. If something is worth around £100K and we can buy it for £50K, if it's in a decent area for rental, but in a bit of a mess right now, we might buy that one to refurbish it and put on the open rental market, then refinance to recycle our cash, so adding another unit to the buy to let portfolio. There might be some cases where it's a larger property with higher values attached, and it would never work as a BTL, but it would make a really nice family home, after a bit of refurbishment TLC. This type of thing might be £150K to buy (as is negotiated with the vendor), require £50K worth of refurb spend on it, then sell on the open market for £300K. In all these scenarios, the owners of the auction house, the ones generating all the leads, are the ones having full control over how these deals are distributed. In our case, we then have the ability to buy for ourselves, trade to a client, list on auction, or list on open market – at all times being in control of how we manage that opportunity.

I do believe that we do this better than anyone, so let's not take that away from us here, as I don't think every auction house operates exactly like us – but they certainly have the ability to, if they were to think like us and set up their operations to deal with matters as I've outlined above. So, maybe like me in my earlier days, perhaps you don't think about auction houses the way they can actually operate. For most auction houses, or anyone that is generating leads for that matter, it would make sense for them to keep the good deals for themselves and trade the ones they don't want. We're slightly different in that regard, since we have obligations to support our clients build their own property businesses, and because we have such a high deal-flow, we are regularly trading what you might call "belter deals" to our clients too. Of course, we still buy for ourselves, but we are also shifting around 30 deals a month to our clients right now as well. There's plenty to go around for everyone involved, and different deals make sense for different people for different reasons. These days it's rare I get to buy a straightforward deal myself, always getting landed with the more complicated ones! But I do like a challenge. And as my saying goes, "I will make money out of this one, somehow!"

One last point on auction houses is to be sure to do your due diligence on any properties you see listed from companies you don't have any relationship with. There's a LOT of sharks out there in this game. Due diligence on the properties is essential, but due diligence on the Articles of Roup and any Special Conditions can be even more important. These are the Terms of

Sale under Auction format and, if not understood correctly, can cost you thousands. There's a whole other market that exists within the auction space where people will buy and sell regularly with crazy terms – and if you don't know what to look for, you will get stung. Obviously if you are a regular buyer and seller yourself, the chances are you will have a decent relationship with whoever you are doing regular business with, and assuming you trust the people of the auction house, it's unlikely they would allow you to be stung, by pointing out any extreme vendor terms before you commit to making a purchase.

So many amateurs lose out big time here – it's a market where these professional auction traders pray on unsuspecting property wannabes that do not understand how the game is played. It might blow your mind and confuse you that this type of activity is even legal, but I assure you it is, and it's actually a strategy for many traders to resell the same property multiple times over, each time taking the deposit value paid by the buyer that was unable to conclude in line with the Terms of Sale. If you imagine a property being sold for £100K, the buyer would need to pay 10%, so £10K as a deposit value, and it's the sellers' right to retain this for failure to conclude in the agreed timeline (typically 28 days, but this can vary by Special Conditions). So if that vendor sells the same property three times, they can make an extra £20K simply from retaining deposits, legally, in line with contract. Bear in mind the auction house, in this example, would take three fees in too, again from this one single property. So be very aware that this game goes on, and in a big way. Know what to look for and you will see the same names cropping up again and again, applying this same strategy. It's not how we roll, in terms of implementing this as a professional trading strategy, albeit the terms are the terms and sellers will retain deposits if buyers fail to conclude in line with whatever terms are agreed.

Not every property in an auction will have some sort of major issue going on. There's a common misperception that if it's in auction it must be falling down or have a major structural defect of some kind. You can find decent deals in auctions now and again, but really all the best deals are off-market. Most deals are in fact done off-market, even if they are listed for auction, as it's just a case of the selling agent trying to find a solution (i.e. an agreeable price) for both the buyer and seller. If a price is successfully negotiated, contracts are exchanged, fees and deposits are paid, then it's into legals for financial settlement. Some auctions still run live in-room auctions with the hammer falling to make a binding contract, but more and more these days the auctions are online and deals are done outside of the traditional auction room environment.

Ultimately, auction houses are lead generation machines, for sellers that are motivated to get rid of their property, and usually quickly too.

Calculators

We have various different types of calculators for when we're analysing any investment opportunities. There's a quick / basic one, a more advanced one, then a separate one for portfolio analysis. I tend to use the advanced one on a day-to-day basis for when we're analysing single units. I say it's advanced, but like anything, it's easy when you know how. It's just a bit more detailed than the basic one, but rapid to analyse a deal for decision making. It is a constantly-evolving document, as we apply new knowledge and experience any time we feel appropriate, but ultimately it's just a Microsoft Excel spreadsheet with data automatically calculated based on the values we insert. For anyone interested in a copy of this, just drop me an email or DM me on socials and I can put you in touch with the team to sort you out with what you need.

The calculators allow for and analyse details such as the following:

- Purchase price
- End value
- ADS % and value
- LBTT (or stamp duty)
- Legal fees
- Sourcing fee
- Refurb budget
- Serviced Accommodation specification & furnishings
- Mears specification & furnishings
- The acquisition funding level
- Whether or not there is any retained interest
  - And how many months are retained, if so
- The acquisition funding interest rate
- The arrangement fee
- Lender legal fees

- Title Indemnity Policy
- The refinance LTV % and consequent value
- The number of months expected before refinance
- The BTL income at point of acquisition, if tenanted
- Letting agent charges at point of acquisition, if applicable
- Insurance costs at point of acquisition
- BTL income after refinance
- Interest rate of term loan
- Letting agent charges after refinance
- Insurance costs after refinance (and tenancy, if not purchased tenanted)
- The expected nightly rate for Serviced Accommodation
- Expected SA occupancy rate %
- SA finance product rate of interest for term loan
- SA management agency costs
- SA booking platform costs
- Insurance costs for operating as SA
- Sales price (if flipped)
- Selling agent costs
- Expected timeline for sale
- Holding finance costs

- Legal fees

- Projected profitability

They are really good tools to very quickly analyse a deal and give you a flavour of how things might pan out. Obviously, you don't know specifics until you've actually bought the deal and gone through the process from start to finish. So many people get caught up on the deal calculator and use certain details to decide on whether or not they will buy. Remember this is a tool to help you analyse but it's not 100% accurate – it never can be front end – and it baffles me why people will turn down a deal based on only receiving £199.99 per month cashflow according to the deal calc. Yet if it cash flowed £200.00 per month, they would be all over it! Analysing deals in your head, or just writing down rough numbers, or maybe missing a couple of details, could be the different between having a successful deal or a problem. It's good practice to use the likes of these templates to make sure you have all the details there ready to complete the analysis – it then gives you all the details you need, every time, to allow you to decide quickly and act accordingly.

Strategies

The main strategies we implement in our business on a daily basis include:

- Buy to let

- Buy to refurb to flip

- Buy to auction flip

- Trade to client

Laurie Duncan @ REWD Group

- Trade to auction

- Trade to open market

All these strategies are implemented with the objective of making money. Don't forget that getting into property means getting into business. It might be stating the obvious here, but a lot of folks think there's some magic golden ticket used to get into property, and yet it's no different from any other business. It takes a lot of hard graft, dedication, and problem solving. There's no point of being in this game if you're not going to create profitability.

Buy to let

The buy to let strategy involves buying the property, always at discount from its true value, refurbing it if necessary, renting it out, refinancing it, then repeating that process. You'll maybe have heard of it as the B-R-R-R strategy. (I've also heard it be called the "BRRRR..." strategy!) However you want to say it and whatever you want to call it, it's all the same stuff. You're buying to keep, benefit from recycling the cash from the refinance, letting the property out to create profit from the rental income, then over time you will also benefit from the capital appreciation, as the property value increases naturally through time. Some will say you can never guarantee the capital appreciation, and whilst that may be true, if you look back through history there is a constant trend of property prices increasing since records began – of course with a few ups and downs in there, but we like the ups and downs because we can make money regardless of the market conditions!

Remember, too, that refinancing is an absolutely sensational way to make lots of tax-free cash – that is different to profit. If you extract a cash value from a refinance that's more than the value of cash you have used in the deal to that point, that, my friend, is tax-free income. Now, let's clarify: it is cash, it is in your bank, but it's not taxable. Cash received to bank in the form of an increased loan is just an increased loan – nothing else. Some of the deal examples I've given throughout this book are great examples of this and, to be honest, this is why I love buy to let on a scale that maybe many others do not understand. It's one thing to create some monthly cashflow – and don't get me wrong, I love that too – but it's another thing to create large lump sums of cash into your business that you can use to continue to grow, without having to pay any tax on those large values of capital created from the buy to let strategy. The refinance process has to be my favourite part of the game – it's so subjective, it's so straightforward, you can really do so, so well out of it, and it can allow you to grow exponentially, and rapidly. When we started out, we were all about buy to let, at massive scale, in rapid time – refinancing is one of the critical parts of that equation.

It's actually pretty crazy to think that people invest in property and build buy to let portfolios without using this strategy. I mean where people just come into money, buy property at market values, then let out and hold for capital appreciation. So much cash locked in, effectively overpaying for properties since not purchased at a discount. If you were to analyse how much a property truly cost if you purchased at market value, it's not actually market value, is it? What about all the other costs that get lumped into your total acquisition costs like ADS, legals, and LBTT if applicable? You would actually probably pay around 110% of the value of an open market property, if you bought at its current home report level – never mind situations where folks are paying over the home report value for a buy to let property! Plus all these other costs. Absolutely bonkers! Buying at discount is critical, no matter what strategy you are implementing. Refinancing to extract that equity created from the discounted purchase is how the PROs do it so quickly. So please, if you're going to do buy to let, do it right. The consequences of not implementing this strategy professionally are very, very expensive.

Buy to refurb to flip

As with any strategy, it will have its pros and cons. When folk are starting out, they always like the idea of doing a property project as a flip with a family member or their best mate or whatever. There's wool over the eyes of everyone involved, not truly calculating the time, the effort, the costs, the applicable taxes, the consequent projected profitability, etc., etc. That mindset does really confuse me, to be honest. That said, so many people don't know what they don't know, and that's just down to lack of exposure to more professional approaches to take. Again, always buy at discount, and that will make things a hell of a lot easier to make some money from the project, even if you did make a royal arse of it.

This strategy allows expression of the interior design flair from the individuals involved! Putting in the fancy new kitchen with the upgraded units, or the fully-tiled bathrooms with the fancy tiles because it looks way nicer that way. Of course, it may be the digital, Bluetooth and probably wi-fi showers, because that would be so much nicer than a basic one. The black contrasting sanitary ware. The LVT flooring. The fully-plastered walls and ceilings. The wallpapered feature walls. The top of the range cooker, dishwasher, hob, sinks. Man – as I write this out, all I can see is loss of profit! Don't get me wrong, there's a time and a place when all this fancy stuff can make sense, but usually it's overkill from inexperienced developers that destroys their profitability.

The biggest issue we've found with this strategy is actually getting the property sold at the end. Open market sales are something we don't do too much of, simply because it's night and day compared to auction terms. When you're selling something on the open market, the sale is not a sale until the final day of settlement, missives are concluded, and the money is in the bank. You will receive offers to buy, hopefully. You will accept the best offer to suit your situation, no doubt. You won't necessarily accept the highest price, as if someone is going to buy cash this should mean they can conclude much quicker. If you did accept the highest price – say it was £10K more – on the face of it, that might seem fantastic, but if that buyer needs to get a mortgage, it will add weeks if not months onto the completion date, and it is entirely possible that this buyer could change their mind, or not get the loan offer they wanted, or find something else, and for some reason pull out of the sale, meaning you're back to square one and sticking the property back on the market again, before repeating the process all over again.

One way to mitigate all the potential aggro when it comes to sale time is to focus on the types of properties that will attract first-time buyers. This type of buyer typically has a deposit ready to go, a loan offer already in place, no chain of other people needing to sell before they can conclude, and a willingness and eagerness to get their purchase concluded quickly. You need to think about refurb spec, which should always be a higher spec than a rental spec, and you will want it to be something that has a *wow* factor when someone walks in, to maximise the chances of getting to a closing date which has the potential to achieve a higher sales price. This stuff is all well and good, but please bear in mind my previous comments regarding crazy overspending and a timeline to get the sale concluded. If a first-time buyer is pushed to the limit financially, they could also end up pulling out after mulling things over during the completion of the legal process – remember, they are not on the line under open market's standard "Offer Terms", and so can pull out at any point with no liability other than maybe some legal costs. Typically, first-time buyers are looking at a lower price range of the market too – maybe up to say £150K or so. Obviously this is dependent on the areas and market at the time, and various other factors of consideration. Comparatively, if you were trying to sell a £1m property to a first-time buyer, you will be aiming for a really narrow part of the market, as most first-time buyers won't have 1) that level of cash to put in, and 2) the ability to obtain funding for a consequent debt level.

Finally, and I might be stating the obvious here, but please consider your corporate structure of any type of this kind of activity. If you're doing it in your own name (or names, if you're doing a JV with a friend or family member), it is classed as trading activity, which is income, which is taxable at your marginal rate of income tax. Back to analysis of the deal in the first place and thinking through the profitability, etc. I'd need to check, but I think the tax would be payable in 90 days from date of settlement if done in personal names. On the other hand, if we consider a Limited Company performing the activity, it could create the profit, hold the cash generated, then not have to pay its Corporation Tax until up to 9 months after the end of the previous accounting period, and it would likely be at a much lesser rate of tax for most, compared to paying it all as income tax.

So, if you're doing buy to refurb to flip as a strategy, please consider all these points I've mentioned above, before going gung-ho into a property project because your mate that has no experience said it would be worth taking a punt on! Note these comments are not exhaustive either, and there will be other things to think about and factor in, but this should give you a good grasp of some of the basics before you make your moves.

Buy to auction flip

Who wouldn't want to buy a property for £20K, then sell it again for £40K one month after purchasing? Well, on the face of it, this is a fantastic strategy, and everyone should do it, so we can all retire to the Bahamas and do property deals from our iPhones, as we sit there on our sun loungers, drinking Mango Margaritas, with the waves lapping against the shore. I've said it before and I'll say it again – this is business, and things will not always go to plan. That being said...! This strategy is also phenomenal and can be highly lucrative, as long as you buy right and choose to acquire a property that will lend itself well to the strategy. There's a lot of different things I really like about this strategy, but the one thing you must factor in, assuming you have finance costs, is the time the property sits on the market before it sells – known as holding costs. These can very quickly mount up and completely change not only the deal dynamic but also the cashflow to the business, and therefore the overall performance of the business.

If you imagine a situation whereby you acquire a property on the 1st of April, then hoped it would sell by the 1st of May, but it doesn't sell (for whatever reason) until the 1st of December, that whole time you have been paying out some kind of finance cost (assuming the purchase was in fact financed), even if it was retaining interest and you had paid it up front. You might be thinking that length of time is fine, and if you still make £20K then it's been worth it in this example. If you're only planning on doing one or two deals per year like them, then maybe you suck it up and maybe that's okay. However, if you imagine this being your whole business model, you would almost certainly be using funding – and if so, when you have 10, or 20, or 50 bits of stock sitting on the market, that is a very dangerous place to be. We have explored this model many times and do actually operate this way, but only as a kind of side strategy to everything else we

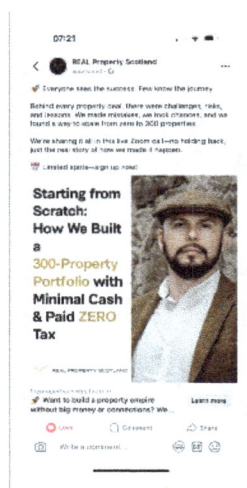

do. The maximum number of units we've had as stock waiting to be sold is 10, but even that tied up a really significant value of cash that we could've been using in other areas of the business. The return has to be worth it, and from our perspective we would consider a 50% return on cash within a six month period as a worthwhile venture. There's no guarantee of timeline with this model, but it works best when the cash goes out the door in month 1 and comes back into the account on month 2.

Selling under Auction Terms gives the buyer and the seller security of contract at the point the hammer falls, the paperwork is signed, or when the payment of a deposit and / or auction fees are paid. The seller is protected if the buyer does not conclude within the contractual timescale, since the deposit value paid by the buyer – which is typically 10% of the purchase price – can be retained by the seller in that event. Also, the seller can then remarket the property for sale. The seller could also legally pursue the previous buyer if they had to accept a lower purchase price from a new buyer, but we rarely see this eventuality. From the buyer's perspective, they have the security of knowing the property is theirs, and nobody else then has the ability to buy it, unless of course the financial settlement does not take place in line with contract, which is typically 28 days from contract commencement date. Notice should be served on the 29th day to confirm from seller to buyer that the deposit will be retained in 7 days if financial settlement doesn't happen, and penalty interest can be charged to the buyer from the seller should they wish to exercise that right. There's then the Special Conditions and these can be wide and varied, so always check if there are any. Of course it's always depending on the situation, but usually both the buyer and the seller are keen to get a deal done, and we as the auction house always try to work with both sides to get it done.

Like all the strategies, though, as long as you buy right, there's always a way to make some money. From our perspective, on this strategy, we can be the buyer, the seller and the auction house, so have various options to monetise any given lead in these different ways.

Trade to client

Straightforward – just as it says on the tin. We get a deal signed up, then pass it to a client for them to buy off-market, directly from the seller. This can be good for sellers and buyers too, since sellers know on day one they have the property sold and should be done within 4-6 weeks, again always depending on specifics of the situation. The buyers, our clients, are happy since they have been brought an investment opportunity directly with no others involved; if they agree to buy it, they pay the sourcing fee, and the deal is theirs. Of course, as part of our support to our clients, we are heavily involved from start to finish, to make sure everyone in the chain is doing their bit to get us to the point of legal conclusion. It's important to note with this strategy, we only ever take deals to our clients that we consider "good enough" for them to buy. If the numbers don't stack as an off-market deal, we don't present them to our clients. Sellers need to know and understand how that side of our business works and if the price isn't attractive enough for one of our clients, we cannot provide that solution to the seller. Obviously this then means that the bigger discounted properties are the ones that our clients are buying.

We make our money from the sourcing fees in this equation. In fact, this is one of our main revenue streams as a business. Sometimes there can be a mixture of strategies in the one deal.

For example, we can trade an off-market deal to a client under auction terms – this could be a requirement of the seller, the buyer, or us as the auctioneer / selling agent. Deal specifics always merit the way deals are done, but sometimes the Terms of Sale are necessary to be controlled, in the interests of all involved.

If you think about it, given our ambitions to be Scotland's Number ONE homebuying company, the only way we can achieve this result is to have a bank of qualified buyers who are experienced, serious, liquid, understand the game, and who are ready to constantly buy these investment opportunities (A.K.A. deals!) from us. Sure, we are buying ourselves, and will continue to do so, but the more buyers we have buying, the more we can spend on marketing, the more leads we can generate, the more deals we can convert, the bigger our clients' businesses will become, and the bigger our business will become too. We work with people for a minimum of two years, to ensure they are educated and experienced enough to continue to buy without any need for support from us. Some people like the support and want to continue paying for that support, whereas others just want to become qualified ASAP and get out there and buy deals, deals, deals! It makes our business infinitely scalable when 1) we have more people we trust as qualified buyers, and 2) we don't need to commit our time to them to support them along the journey, as they've already done the legwork to get their property business off the ground to the point where it will take care of itself, which can happen in the background if clients are focusing on other business ventures, or travelling, or whatever else they might be involved in. If you want to become a qualified buyer and get access to all the types of deals I'm going on about, drop me a message and we can get a call arranged to discuss how we might do some business together.

III

Trade to auction

This strategy is useful for when we don't want to buy it or trade it ourselves – usually if the discount level isn't big enough for us to consider as an investment opportunity, for us or our clients. The sellers usually select auction as their preferred solution if they are happy to hold out for a while and see what interest they get, to hopefully get a higher sales value. It is common, though, over time, for sellers to change their views and reduce their expectations on achievable purchase price, in most cases being led by the market and the lack of interest in that particular piece of stock. So sometimes a piece of auction stock can turn into a deal over time, if the seller chooses to bring their price down to be more in line where it could work as a deal for our clients.

In this day and age there's not so many auctions doing live in-room auction format sales. There are a few, but this would be considered the more traditional method. Selling under auction terms doesn't have to be in an auction room, nor does it need to be on auction day. If a buyer wants to buy and a seller wants to sell, the deal can be done on any day at any time. It's the terms of the auction that give buyer and seller the security, as discussed previously. So it's very common to have auction stock being traded throughout the month as drip-fed revenue from the auction fees, rather than a big dump of revenue on auction day, as most people might perceive. Auction day is awesome, though – there's a real buzz about the office. It tends to be a later night for the staff, with some decent food brought into office and a big focus on doing deals. I'm rarely involved in it directly, but I do feel there's a different vibe in the office on auction day. So much potential sits with us between the buyers and sellers – the staff are off and on the phones, constantly working on both sides of the deal, with lots of revenue on the table for the business and commissions on the table for the staff.

I'd say the biggest takeaway from this strategy is for you to realise that the deals sitting online in auction houses tend to be the types of deals that aren't good enough to consider as investment opportunities. Off-market deals are where it's at, all day long. If a deal was really good enough for investors to buy, it would've been bought already. Not every auction house operates the way we do though, with our multiple exit strategies, so be aware of that and recognise that many auction houses will list stock after stock after stock, and end up with a shit tonne of stock online available for sale, but only ever selling a small portion of that. We tend to focus on quality over quantity. Throwing shit against a wall and hoping it sticks, has never been something we want to do as a business. Again, we're focused on helping people grow their property businesses, and so prefer to focus on what we know is good. I dread to think how much time is wasted from these guys out there that just list stock for the sake of listing it – they must carry so much dead weight! So if you are looking for quality deals, we can definitely help you with that.

Trade to open market

This is basically just estate agency business. Listing stock online for sale, taking enquiries, dealing with a bit of admin, not so much strategic selling involved in this strategy. We don't do so much of this. We do it now and again where it makes sense for us to do so, but really the revenues from this type of business activity are not interesting to us. It's not considered worthwhile, when we compare it to our other revenue streams and the profitability of off-market and auction trades. It's funny, though – as I write this now, we've literally just been discussing this situation in a strategy day between the Directors, about how we should maybe bring on some staff to start doing a bit more estate agency stuff. We go back and forth on it. Really, the thought process comes from all the leads we're generating now but not doing anything with – these are all people looking to sell their homes, and we tend to dismiss the majority of these leads when we could be monetising them, somehow. Whether it's staff we should bring in or agencies we should partner with, it probably is something we should have a degree of involvement in.

For now, we don't do a lot of it, but I guess I can say to watch this space, as I imagine we will scale up this side of the business in the coming year or so – once we've moved into our fancy new office gaff in Glasgow!

Refurbs

A lot of folk think about doing property deals where refurbs are essential to get an uplift in value. Let me tell you right now and very directly here, that is NOT the case. Just by buying at a discount is where you make your money. There's probably a 70/30 split in terms of deals we do with refurbs or without. If a property is worth £100K and you can buy it for £70K, there's no refurb required, and you can just simply immediately refinance it against its true value of £100K. So why would you want to mess about with time and cost of a refurb? If this concept is challenging for your mind to accept, it's purely down to your lack of experience in the game. I love deals where there is no refurb required! So simple. So satisfying. So quick to recycle cash. Okay, there's no self-gratification to test out your Homes Under the Hammer ambitions, or no fancy wallpaper feature wall, or no upgraded fancy bathroom or kitchen with contrasting handles, but really – who gives a flying fuck about all that?! This is a numbers game. If you can refinance, recycle cash, rent it out, then buy another unit, and repeat this process over and over again and again, why would you not want to do that? You would. And you should! Trust me – focus on the numbers and you will do very, very well.

Obviously, there are occasions where you will need to refurb. Particularly if you're doing a buy to refurb to flip – and yes, these will be the fancier ones where you can put your sparkle on the finishings. Refurbs are an essential part of all these strategies and you definitely will need to do them along your journey. They will come in different shapes and sizes – the basic ones, the big ones, the mid-range ones, the ones with the roof issues, the wee mini ones, the kitchen-only ones, the ones with the damp, the ones with the woodworm, the ones with the needles, the ones with the faeces, the ones with the stair lifts, the ones where you thought it would only be £5K and it ended up £20K... The list goes on and on. Nothing fazes me on refurbs now, purely down to having "seen it all" over our short time, so far! Again, I focus purely on numbers, and each unit will be what it will be in terms of whatever we find under the carpet as we get into a refurb.

One essential part of the refurb element of your business is to have a good, reliable, national network of trades, that will help you out with whatever it is you need done. We made so many mistakes at the start of our journey when it comes to refurbs. Ideally you want to deal with one person that will facilitate the whole job, including all the different people and trades you need involved, so you can engage with that one person and they control everything from start to finish. Really, though, these guys are hard to come by, I've found – especially with the type of refurb works you will be doing. It's not like you are refurbishing or constructing big new fancy houses – the works will likely be done in smaller flats and houses, sometimes in a really bad condition, so the working conditions for the trades aren't always ideal. Even if you can find a single person to be your go-to for the refurb works, they might be a "yes-man" and tell you "yes" to every question you ask, and they may be the type of person to take on work as an apparent all-trades supplier, but when they get into the guts of the work their usual team of people let them down and it can end up a bit of a mess. We are very fortunate to have Holly "HLH" Hodgson as our in-house project manager now in REAL Property Scotland, and she does actually take care of all the individual trades on behalf of our clients. Since we operate nationally across Scotland, and provide a good, steady stream of work to our team of external tradesmen, we find we can very effectively and efficiently take care of any kind of refurb project. From your perspective, you want to get in and out of the deal ASAP, so you can move on and purchase your next one. An efficient refurb allows you to do that.

Phase 1 V Phase 2

The types of deals you will do in what we call Phase 1 will be very different to Phase 2. Phase 1 sees the business get up and running, doing single unit deals, one after the other, to build a solid base of assets and prove the model. Once the business is established and generating some decent cashflow, we can start to think about levelling up, into what we call Phase 2. Phase 2 sees the implementation of more deals on the go at any one time, and more complex deals thrown into the mix too. Again, if you focus on raising money and buying deals, you will create a successful property business by default. More complex deals might be the type of deal that others, due to their lack of experience or the early stage in their own journey, might shy away from as they view it as 'too risky', and that might be a reasonable view for people to take when they're just starting out. Your views will likely change as you grow, though, as you obtain more experience deal by deal, allowing you to take a different approach and get involved in deals with a higher risk profile. Chances are you wouldn't do a portfolio deal as your first ever property deal, for example, and even if you did have that opportunity it might not be the right thing for you to do, since it's prudent to cut your teeth before going gung-ho into a portfolio deal, which is a whole other level of complexity versus single unit deals. Phase 2 allows you the ability to take on these more complex deals, potentially structuring deals using more advanced combinations of financial strategy, and giving you an advantage over many others that will be stuck in Phase 1, with most investors not even recognising there is a difference between these two (what we call) Phases. If you think about it, most landlords aren't even learning the financial strategies, never mind the deal acquisition strategies, and it's the combination of both that separates the PROs, such as yourself, from the amateurs.

It was a fascinating statistic for me to learn that the majority of landlords only actually own one single rental property. The average number of units owned per landlord across the UK is apparently three units. Now I don't know about you, but one unit or three units just does not cut it for me. I cannot understand why anyone would even mess about with things if massive scale is not on the radar. Now, I say massive scale, and I appreciate that might not be everyone's bag, but surely if we're talking – rental portfolio wise – that you would want at least, say, 20 units? 20 units at around £300 average cashflow per month equals around £6K per month (appreciating this is before voids, arrears and maintenance, and any other operational costs, but that's the point...). In order to live off your portfolio, you'll need to have a figure of around at least £5K per month of cash, surely. Anything less than that, in my opinion, is a very risky place to be. Obviously, if you're not living off the property income, and you have the property business as a side hustle, you can have any amount building up in the background, then the figure isn't so critical. But in my view it's always better to have more units, as the cashflow from the successful operational units can always cover any voids, arrears and maintenance from any problematic units.

Imagine a month where you're just starting out, you're in Phase 1, and you maybe do your first deal, then it could be another few months before you do another deal. You might get to, say, five units in your first year. This is just to set the scene – I appreciate every story will be different. Some folks might take six months to do their next deal, and others might do three deals in their first six months. Maybe even to get to five units in your first year would be a huge deal for you! In that case, please start and start now, as you will achieve that goal with your eyes shut! Then you think comparatively about a scenario in Phase 2, where every single month you are buying a single unit. It's almost like having completed an apprenticeship in Phase 1, if you want to use that analogy. So you're in Phase 2 now, and every month you are doing a deal – man, that is seriously rapid growth. And no, you won't ever stop either – trust me! Buying property deals is like eating a packet of Pringles.

So, we're now in this Phase 2 segment of our journey and deals are flying in. We have credibility, we have investor cash coming in regularly, we are buying to let, buying to flip, buying to SA, trading deals we don't want to other investors, and now we're starting to look at doing our first residential portfolio deal as well as considering commercial deals. Oh yes, oh yes, oh yes – now things are fairly ramping up and it's getting proper exciting. We are professional property investors now! But the whole feel of business is very different in this Phase 2. The likelihood is that you will be full-time in property by this point, unless of course you love your day job, or you're getting away with murder and milking the employment income. Phase 2 is just this beautiful place of deal-harmony with deals getting done right, left and centre, and your business is booming away in the background without you having to think too much about it.

To finish off this section of deals using the terminologies of Phase 1 versus Phase 2, let me give you an example of a live deal we have on the go in REWD Developments Limited, our trading company. It is an absolute belter, and will probably end up being one of the best deals we've ever done. That said, we're still working through the process, and it's not fully exited as yet. For most folk reading this book, they will probably appreciate this is very much a Phase 2 type deal, rather than something to be taken on within the Phase 1 section of the property investment journey. The project itself is actually split into 2 sections too though, and even if section 2 wasn't to go ahead (which I don't think will be the case at all), section 1 is actually a belter of a deal in itself, however you skin the cat here.

So, this deal is on LaPorte Precinct in Grangemouth, and is a commercial property. Grangemouth Precinct, for anyone that doesn't know, is in my local area. There's a real lack of investment generally, no support from the Council whatsoever, and I think we are the only ones that are actively trying to bring back some footfall and economy to the place. It's like a small High Street, but I wouldn't even go as far to call it that – it's really just a small street with some empty shops. Some may see only the negatives in these previous comments, but of course, as always, I only see opportunities...!

For the unit we acquired, there's a small shopfront on the downstairs section which is around 45 square metres, with a large empty office section upstairs around 300 square metres in size. It was on the open market for £150K. We, "cheekily", offered £60K. Why? Well, because our intention was to split off the shop on to its own title, and do same with upstairs space, let the shop out on its own, then convert the upstairs space into a 12-bedroom HMO, with the costs of the conversion expected to be around £300K as budgeted (as we advised to the selling agent). The end value of the HMO would likely be £25K per room, meaning £300K GDV on that part. The shop would be what it would be, but expected value on that was maybe around £60K based on a rent around £500 per month. So a projected £360K GDV on the total project, with our costs being £300K development and £60K purchase price. These figures are what drive our purchase price down, and the sellers could get on board with that. Also, like I already mentioned, there's not so many people looking to invest in this area, so we were in a strong purchasing position because of that. Then, combined with our credibility for sticking to our word and getting deals done, the sellers were sure we would proceed with the deal, should we come to an agreement on the purchase price. Now, they did not accept our cheeky £60K offer! But they did counter at £65K, and we gladly accepted! I've said it before and I'll say it again – there are belter deals everywhere. (Yes, that's both on and off-market...)

So we had it valued for funding on the acquisition, obtained a vacant possession valuation based on a sale within 180 days of, you guessed it, £65K – bang on the money. This property was actually on the market for six months, or 180 days, and literally anyone could've bought it. Funding for the acquisition was at 70% of the 180-day value, so we had to put in around £35K of cash, allowing for deposit cash and the usual fees and costs that go along with a purchase. I referred previously to this deal being split into two sections. Section 1 was to split off the downstairs shop and have it on its standalone title with no connection to the upstairs space, as was the case previously when we acquired. So, we put a wall up to split the access of the two units – upstairs V downstairs – and then it was time to rent out the downstairs shop and get some rental income coming in, as well as refinance in entirety, and title split at this stage in the process too. Having the shop on its own title and the upstairs space on its own separate title, meant we would have much greater flexibility when it was to come to finance options for both of them. Having an unencumbered development space, rather than it being tied in with funding with an existing commercial investment unit (i.e. the shop), is always a better way to work it, if you can deal with that through legals.

I expected we would get £1K per month of rent on the shop, so £12K rent per annum, but was told by the marketing agent that would be too pricey – he thought more like £8K per annum, and was concerned that if we went in too expensive, we might alienate some of the market from even enquiring. We had a bit of back and forth on this, but ultimately agreed to market the shop at a rental value of £9K per annum. It was no shock to me that we had multiple interested parties within the first week of the property going live! So in my opinion, the rent was still too low. Anyway, we got interest, got to analyse the potential tenancy profiles, and elected to go with a barber, as we felt he would be the best tenant for a few different reasons. Typically in the commercial world, of course always subject to the strength of the covenant (covenant being fancy commercial property speak for the tenant type and length of lease), you can achieve a 10 times multiplier on the rent as your market valuation for the property. Maybe you can also see here now why I was keen on the higher rental income? If we got a tenant at £9K per year, I'm expecting a valuation of £90K on the shop. If we got them signed up at £12K per year, I'm expecting a £120K valuation on the shop. Bear in mind this is just the small shop we're talking about here – the development space upstairs would shortly become unencumbered (i.e. no secured debt attached to it). The barber was teed up and happy to proceed, but I really thought the rent should've been higher, as I mentioned earlier, so I called the barber tenant directly to explain this and confirmed to him that if he can work with us at the £12K rent, we would be happy to bring him on as the tenant. He duly obliged. A five-minute phone call to achieve not just an extra three grand a year in rent, but also an expected uplift in value of £30K on the property, with the expectation that we would obtain 70% of the valuation in secured funding against the shop, which would consequently equate to another £20K odds of cash out of the deal for us, at the refinance stage. I hope this is making sense to you, and you can see just how beautifully this game can be played.

As I write this, the valuation was done a week or two ago, and the £120K valuation on the wee shop was formally confirmed. Now we sit back and wait for the legals to conclude on that side before we get into the upstairs space for development. Just in case you missed it earlier, we purchased this whole building for £65K, and we just received a £120K valuation on the shop alone, not including the development space. I've said it before and I'll say it again – I absolutely LOVE finance and refinances. It is incredible what you can achieve when you know how to play this game professionally. The longer the lease, the stronger the covenant when it comes to commercial terms too, so it helped us in this case that the tenant would sign a deal at a 10-year lease length. There's a rolling break after 3 years, in case either party wants to terminate, but in this example it had no impact on the valuation and / or the funding.

But I keep going on and on about this little shop – what about the upstairs development space? Well, since we acquired the building, we've been going back and forth with architects and the Council, assessing what the action plan should be on that element of the project. Initially, we created a design based on operating it as an HMO, but received negative feedback from the Planning Department after they consulted with the HSE. Considering we already have another three HMOs in this street, all within around 300 metres of each other, you will be as confused as me to hear that they wouldn't be supportive of another one, based on this feedback from the HSE. Nothing to do with concentricity of HMOs or concerns over our ability to operate them or anything else, but the HSE's guidance was that it would be a safety concern to have this unit as an HMO. I was confused, to say the least. From our side though, as professional property investors, we just want to buy the properties, refurbish if necessary, and let them out to collect the rental income. We really don't care about how the unit is actually licensed or operates, as long as we can rent out the rooms. So you might be even more confused to hear that we couldn't operate the unit as an HMO, due to safety concerns of it being in the blast zone of the INEOS petrochemical facility (I know, don't even get me started – there's around 10,000 homes in Grangemouth in this blast zone already). So an HMO was a no-go, and we started to look at alternative designs, layouts, and ways to operate the building. Whilst it was a no to an HMO, what would work well is a hotel! (Apparently.) Same number of rooms, rooms being let out to collect rental income, refinancing against the strength of the covenant (as and when we get someone signed onto a lease), so all the same shit from our perspective.

There are a couple of considerations, though, in terms of the difference between building and operating the unit as either a residential premises or a commercial premises. A residential premises being a "house" of multiple occupation, and a commercial premises being the hotel. I actually thought, before going through the process of this project, that you needed an operational licence to run a hotel – it turns out you only need licencing if you're operating a bar, and we do not like to complicate things in REAL Property Scotland! So there will be no booze sold, therefore we will not need any kind of licence. There is a boozer directly underneath this unit, and there's an ASDA right across the road if the tenants fancy a few cans of an evening. A few points to think about when it comes to a commercial development project, rather than a residential project, are:

- Residential:
  - Higher LTV exit funding (typically up to 75%)

- o Higher costs of development due to higher specification of a residential build

- o Licencing requirements

- o Lower costs of term loan funding (currently around 6% APR)

- o Comparables used for valuation (and there's usually not many 12-bedroom resi properties that have been sold, never mind sold in the last few months!)

- Commercial:

  - o Lower LTV exit funding (typically up to 70%)

  - o Lower costs of development

  - o No licencing, assuming you are operating the unit without any licencing requirements

  - o Higher costs of term loan funding (usually around 10% APR)

  - o Market analysis will be taken into account but a Covenant could be used for valuation (which can be highly advantageous depending on how you tenant the property)

So we're waiting on planning approval for the hotel design, and we expect to obtain that within Q2/Q3 of 2025. We fully expect to secure 100% development funding on the upstairs space, with a budgeted development spend of around £250K, meaning we shouldn't need to put any cash into that side of the project. If we do, it will be minimal. Again, having this development space on its own title and unencumbered, really helps us with flexibility of funding options here. End value expected to be around £300K for the upstairs space, although we will push for £30K per room and there's 12 rooms in the design, meaning GDV would be £360K on that basis. Time will tell how all that pans out but of course we have ideas as to how to tenant the property at 100% occupancy. End result should be though, that we have 12 rooms all let at a minimum of £150 per room per week, with expectations being more like £180 per room per week, potentially even £200 per room per week. Rental income then is projected to be anywhere between:

- £150 * 12 rooms * 52 weeks / 12 months = £7,800 per month

- £180 * 12 rooms * 52 weeks / 12 months = £9,360 per month

- £200 * 12 rooms * 52 weeks / 12 months = £10,400 per month

This deal should be an all money out deal in a maximum of two years, if not at the point of upstairs refinance, with around £150K equity created (that's around £120K on hotel plus around £30K on shop), with some serious cashflow coming in once the hotel deal is done. Section 2 is as equally glorious as section 1, I hope you will agree, but both with their own elements of excellence and lucrative fruitions.

We are probably better known for our Phase 2-style residential portfolio deals rather than these types of commercial development projects, but I thought this was a really good example to provide in the book so you can get a flavour for what else is out there. Remember, we purchased this on the open market. We've not done anything fancy here. We're not some special breed that's doing anything out of the ordinary. We simply saw an opportunity (on the open market), assessed it, discussed creative solutions as to how best to deal with the various elements of the project, then put a plan in place to create a success out of that. Fair to say, though, that there's no way we could've done this type of project when we were initially starting out, and it has taken a lot of different experiences to get us to the stage where we are confident and capable to handle the complexities involved here. Anyone can do it, though, and that's obviously what we support our clients with too. For people starting out on their property journeys, we help facilitate that, guaranteeing to get their first deal done and their property business up and running, assuming they will follow our guidance and bring (or raise!) the necessary cash value to buy. There's no question that our level of experience – because of all our efforts to date, even from the building company days – has now started to pay dividends, and that can be the same for you too, if you take that first step.

Maybe you're not just starting out. Maybe you've already done a few deals and have some properties under your belt. It's actually quite common for this client type to start to work with us too, as they've realised through reading books like this that there's another world out there. So many folk still have properties in their own names too, as they've maybe not had the right support or guidance when starting out initially. I think it's natural to think you can do it all yourself without any support from more experienced others. I can relate to that too – always taking things said with a pinch of salt, and thinking I could create a better result by not following certain elements of the process and just going about things my own way. Well, I guess we've muddled through! (Thankfully...) But so many mistakes can be avoided with a bit of experience thrown into the mix. So much time can be saved. Ultimately, so much money can be saved simply from investing some capital into education, support, mentorship, community, trainings, and experiences, from the start. I'm a big advocate of that. Back in the day when I was getting started, I would go up and down the UK attending events, seminars, and paid for courses, to learn about all things property and mindset related – those were the two areas I believed would give me the necessary skills to create a success in a property-related business. I still believe that to this day. Obviously, through "doing", we can learn a lot too, but I do think that mindset and strategy are the two fundamentals of business – without investing in those areas, I don't think we would be where we are now.

Whether you're just starting out, or you're already up and running but need to refine your model before you scale it up, or you're maybe a business owner already with some decent capital behind you and you want to get serious about building an additional income stream without shelling out tonnes of your profits to the taxman, this is exactly what we do in REAL Property Scotland. You might like single unit resi deals, you maybe want to focus on portfolio deals, or maybe you just want to go after the more creative commercial style deals that I've touched on in this section of the book. Well, our deal flow is phenomenal, and it's only increasing as we scale our business. If you want to tap into that, drop me a message and let's get a call setup to discuss how we might do some business together. I absolutely LOVE helping other people achieve what they maybe once thought was impossible! I used to believe that too, and now look what we have going on. *In-credible.*

REAL PROPERTY
INVESTORS

FINANCE

Unlimited Money

When you hear a statement like "unlimited money", it might challenge your mind to even accept that the principle is possible – and I get that. I never used to believe it myself. Again, I can only talk from my own experience here, as well as knowing literally hundreds (if not thousands) of others who have implemented these same finance strategies in their own businesses, whether that's a property business or any other business for that matter, but UN-LIMITED MONEY IS EVERYWHERE. First step, believe it's possible. Second step, go out there and get it.

In this section of the book I'm going to talk a bit about *alllll* the different types of finance you can access to bring into your property business. You'll all have heard of by now, I assume, and I did mention it briefly already in an earlier chapter: Other Peoples' Money (or OPM as it's abbreviated to). I've done a separate section within the Finance chapter to talk through private investors, and all that goes along working with them, as these people are the ones who will fund your financially free lifestyle, that I assume you seek. Believe me, that freedom is out there, but you must work for it. So I'll cover private investors separately, albeit that category really is only one of the endless financial strategies you can use.

I've maybe said it before, but finance is without doubt my favourite part about the whole business thing, not even necessarily specific to property, but when you understand finance, how it works, and how you can use it to your massive advantage, THEN combine that with buying properties at big discounts from their true values, I hope you can see how simplistic it can be to make some serious financial gains from the implementation of this strategy.

At this stage, I'm going to list some of the many ways you can raise funds to bring cash into your business, all of which we have done and continue to do, and all with their own pros and cons of use, which I'll also expand on briefly category by category:

- Private investors

- Home equity

- Credit cards

- Bank loans

- Commercial funders

- Bridging companies

- SSAS pensions

- Trading company performance funding

- Corporate loans

- Gifted funds

- Inheritance

- Sale of assets

- Mezzanine funders

- Mortgages

- Joint Venture partners

- Crowd funding

- Vendor finance

- Government grants

- Your own liquidity / savings

- Overdrafts

- Challenger banks

Private investors:

For private investors, I've covered this in much more detail in the section after this. Private investors are so fundamental to your growth – they are the people who provide the key to your unlimited income potential. They deserve their own space within the Finance section of the book!

Home equity:

An example could be a property that's worth £500K, with an existing mortgage balance on it of £200K. Typically, banks will give you, on your home, mortgages up to 85% LTV. 85% of £500K is £425K, so if you remortgaged your home, you could get access to £425K-200K = £225K! A lot of folks don't even realise they are in this position, and there's a lot of people sitting on a lot of equity.

Obviously you need to make sure you can afford the increase in the debt, but if you loan that equity release to your company, then have your company paying you back a standing order to cover the increased cost, as long as your property business gets to the point where it's creating enough cash to firstly cover that extra cost, then secondly to create profit from that cost, then it's been a worthwhile exercise.

This could be your own home equity, or it could be the equity of others, that can borrow for example at 5% APR, lend to you at 10% APR, which could create a win-win scenario for both your private funder using their home equity, and your property business that would now be liquid with cash.

Credit cards:

Probably my favourite finance strategy. I don't know anywhere else you can borrow money for 0% APR, unless it's gifted to you. Sometimes there's minimal fees associated with using credit cards, and they're typically anywhere from 1%-4% of the value of the requested debt, but sometimes these fees don't even exist.

The best card I've ever come across is a Santander credit card, where you can borrow up to 95% of your credit limit on a balance transfer, for 28 months, at 0% APR interest rate, and a 0% transaction fee. This means that you can literally borrow that money without zero cost whatsoever. As long as you pay the debt off before the promotional rate expires, you will have FREE MONEY! Unbelievable, yet believable, because it exists.

Some cards are better than others – I prefer to use **www.moneysupermarket.com** to analyse options, as they let you know what you're pre-approved for before you even apply – and each card can have different 0% offers on one of the three ways you can use the credit:

1) *Purchases*

As it says on the tin. Buying products or services from a supplier, using your credit card to do so.

2) *Balance Transfers*

Transferring money from one card to another. Most cards work this way, but there are some exceptions to be aware of, such as American Express and any kind of Charge Card (those are not considered 'credit cards' by many of the mainstream providers).

3) *Money Transfers*

Literally transfers cash into your bank account, for you to use on whatever you want.

Please promise me though, that you will only use credit cards for building your asset base! Remember, to quote Robert Kiyosaki's *Rich Dad Poor Dad*, "assets put money in your pocket, liabilities take money from your pocket." Please, please, please only use credit (or any other form of finance) to build your asset column. If you use credit cards to buy liabilities, you've used a liability to fund a liability, and that is never going to end well.

Another benefit of using credit cards, aside from how cheap they are to borrow with, is that you only need to make the minimum payments each month, which are usually around 1% of the amount borrowed, albeit each card is different. This massively helps cashflow, as you only have marginal payments to pay out, as you grow the income of your property business.

Many people say that you can't buy properties using credit cards, but you definitely can, and we've done it multiple times.

Money transfer, cash in bank, leverage with other types of funding if necessary... job done!

Bank loans:

Another really quick and easy way to access funding, but it comes at costs of 1) typically around 10% APR for unsecured personal loans, as well as 2) a relatively high regular monthly payment since they are usually around five year repayment profiles. Example of a £50K bank loan is approx £1K per month repayment, impacting more heavily on your cashflow, compared to the likes of the credit card option.

One really important point on bank loans is that if they are secured, meaning there would be a registered legal charge registered on the relevant land register of the property, and note security is typically requested for loans above £50K, then that would likely inhibit your ability to then use home equity, assuming you have an existing 1st Charge lender, and the bank loan would then become a 2nd Charge lender.

Commercial funders:

There can be a crossover in terminologies between "commercial funders" and "bridging funders" (note: bridging explained in next section), since commercial funders typically also offer bridging funds as one of their many product offerings. We would consider a "commercial funder" as any private bank that has appetite to be more flexible in exchange for higher costs, which are of course relative to the risk the bank would take; for example at higher LTPPs (loan to purchase price ratio) or LTVs (loan to value ratio).

Some commercial funders only offer bridging, others only term loans, others various other "product types", but I guess the distinction is that these types of companies are very different from the likes of High Street Banks (HSBs). HSBs typically have a LOT of corporate red tape and they usually look for the borrowers to put in more cash and upfront too, whereas the commercial type operations will have much more quirky and flexible offerings, sometimes allowing no cash (or certainly very minimal cash) required to be put into the deal.

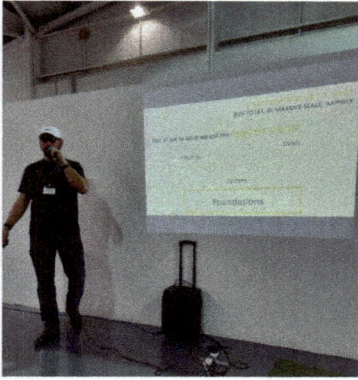

Bridging companies:

Short term flexible cash. Can lend on four walls with no roof on an empty piece of land! In theory...

Bridging companies typically offer up to 90% of the purchase value, taking a 1st Charge Security, with rates around 1% per month (or 12% APR). Usually loans are for 12 months, with a 6 month extension by agreement and subject to an extension fee. Sometimes a survey is required but it can be the case that desktop valuations are accepted in lieu, subject to lender policy and the actual level of net LTV % they are funding.

We talk about two stages of a deal – acquisition and exit. The acquisition is just to buy the property. The exit can be to refinance and hold to let and generate rental income, or to sell it on to make money that way. Bridging cash is always used at acquisition stage, and you want to get off the bridge ASAP.

Many people think of bridging as "expensive money". In my opinion that's a flawed way to think about it. Bridging, for me, allows you to massively leverage your cash position and buy multiple units with the same pot of funds. Would you rather have 10 units or 3 units? 10 every time for me – the more you scale, the more coverage you have, and bridging allows that scale to happen. Worth every penny! "Expensive" or otherwise.

SSAS pensions:

If you're new to property, you've maybe never even heard of a SSAS – it stands for Small Self-Administered Scheme. It's basically a pension for business owners that allows up to 11 members – they're like SIPPS (Self Invested Pension Plans), but a lot more flexible. With a SSAS, you can buy land, commercial property, or you can loan the funds out to either your own businesses or to external parties – it basically puts you in a degree of control around your pension funds, albeit administered by a professional Trustee that ensures you are at all times acting within the restrictions of the HMRC legislation.

We've found that there's a massive degree of disparity between SSAS Administrators – some will say it's okay to do certain things and others not. Some will allow unsecured loans and others not. That said, when loaning funds to your own entities, or any Connected Party for that matter, there are restrictions on that around 1) the amount you can lend yourself and 2) the necessity for some kind of security provision.

And no, you can't use your pension for anything you can get any kind of enjoyment out of: fancy cars, fine wine, whisky, a private jet, etc.!

SSASs get mixed reviews nowadays – it's an unregulated space and there's a lot of folks that say they know pensions but have never had any experience with a SSAS, so it can lead to controversy around what can and cannot be done. My simplistic view of SSASs, though, is that if you're in business and you're in property, you should seriously consider getting one, as there's a tonne of legitimate tax advantages to having this type of operation in your corporate arsenal.

Back when we got started, there were a lot of people getting into SSAS and using those funds to lend out to private companies for a return, rather than leaving it sitting with an investment business that would simply invest funds on your behalf and hope for the best that you would generate a return! What we've found is that the SSAS space has changed a bit in our time, and we don't hear about it so often now. That said, my view remains that it should be a serious consideration for anyone involved in the business space that is also involved in property.

Trading company performance funding:

There are lots of funders out there that like lending to trading entities. There's not necessarily any security consideration, apart from PGs (Personal Guarantees) which seem to be quite a typical request. There's short-term funding and long-term funding options, and these funders will look at the turnover of your trading entity, then – depending on the strength of your business – will offer terms to allow you to take out significant loans. These loans can then be gifted (or loaned) to your property investment business and used to massively scale.

We've done this ourselves very successfully, and have educated many others on how to implement this strategy too. Obviously you need to have a successful trading business to access these funds, as well as being able to cashflow the loan repayments, but the funders wouldn't fund you if they didn't think that was possible. If necessary, you can repay the funds from your property investment company (PIC), back to your trading company, but it's a better cashflow situation for your PIC if it doesn't need to factor in these loan repayments – it will improve cashflow and allow you to scale your PIC faster, as it will have a larger surplus of available funds to combine with other forms of acquisition finance.

To clarify this finance solution, as an example:

- Trading entity borrows £250K

- Trading entity gifts or loans £250K to PIC

- PIC now has £250K cash in bank

- PIC uses the £250K cash as "deposit cash", combines it with bridging finance

- PIC buys 10 units in first year of operating

- Trading entity finances the loan repayments, so PIC cashflow unaffected

- End result is a monster portfolio in a very short period of time

Corporate loans:

We've been fortunate enough to meet lots of supercool entrepreneurs in our time, with a variety of different business types across all sectors. There's a lot of successful people with decent cash pots that are always looking to diversify their investment portfolio. In the example above, of trading company performance funding, this scenario involves you loaning funds from your own trading entity to your own PIC.

Other corporations (people!) sitting with surplus cash in their business bank account, might want to start their own PIC. But also, depending on how much surplus cash they have, and their attitude to risk, they might also want to loan funds out to other PICs, such as yours! We've found that most folk do like diversification, and will consequently like a blended approach where they do both of the previously mentioned options – that's start their own PIC as well as look to loan funds out for a return on cash with no work involved. So this scenario is where one company lends to another. It can be a great way to raise lots of cash to grow your business. There's a lot more people out there that have a lot more money than you think, by the way, but when it comes to businesses (rather than people), the businesses are the places to find much larger sums of cash. Start with people, then as your credibility grows, you can kick off conversations with some business owners. You might be quite surprised at how many are keen to support you, by taking you up on your offering.

Gifted funds & DSC:

Gifted funds, whether from one of your own corporate entities, or whether from family or friends, are a great source of funds – who doesn't want some free money?! The beauty of gifted funds are that they attract no liability. Now, that might sound like a very obvious statement, but when we come to analyse DSC (Debt Service Cover) at the point of using gifted funds together with bridging finance, for example, which does attract a liability, i.e. the cost of funds, gifted funds have no impact there.

Compare a gifted funds scenario to a private investor unsecured loan scenario, with the latter attracting 10% APR of cost. That cost gets factored into the bridging funder's financial analysis of your ability to pay 1) the interest due to them and 2) the actual loan repayment itself at the end of the term. What you will find is that there can be reductions in LTVs, ultimately the funds loaned to you, meaning you need to put in more cash than you initially projected.

Typically bridging funders will offer a "retained interest" facility, rather than a "serviced interest" facility, when there are additional costs to factor in, or if the borrower has poor affordability, or if the borrower is generally not financially sound. Retained interest is typically 12 months' worth of interest, paid up front to the lender, which ultimately reduces the net loan funds you will receive from them. Serviced interest is usually obtainable if you're buying a property that is already tenanted, regardless of the financial status of the borrower, since the rental income coming in covers the cost of the acquisition funding. This is always subject to application to funder, of course, but we have never actually experienced a situation where a buyer has not been able to obtain any funds.

Gifted funds = no cost = no impact on the DSC calcs.

I guess I should probably also explain how DSC actually works... Say a lender has a stress test rate of 150%, which is high, but it's what we've been stressed at in the past, so it's worthy of an example here. Obviously whenever you're looking at your own lending options, you can simply vary the % value of the calculation to generate your desired result.

So, if we take a mortgage interest cost of say £500 per month, then multiply that value by 150%, the answer is £750 per month. In order for you / the borrower to have appropriate debt service cover (DSC), you must have a rental income of a minimum of £750 in order to comply with this aspect of the lender's criteria. If, for example, you only had a rental income of £700 per month, the lender would then look to reduce the amount of borrowing they provide to you, since your DSC is lower than their stress test rate. Now, like I said, the rate of 150% is high, but generally speaking if you pass 150% you will always be fine lending wise, which is why I like to use it as a calculation value. If your rental income was say £500 per month, and the stress test rate was 150%, this would effectively mean the bank would only offer you funding that cost £333 per month, in order to remain within their criteria.

If we look at this as an example in terms of actual numbers, we can consider as follows:

If we have a property valued at £100K, and take out a 75% LTV mortgage, we will have a debt value of £75K. If the funding has an interest rate of 6% APR, this means a finance cost of £375 per month. This calculation is to simply take the debt value of £75K, multiply it by the 6% APR finance cost, then divide that number by 12 months to get the monthly relative finance cost. If we have a stress test rate of 150%, this means we need to multiply the £375 by 150% to get our level of DSC, which gives an answer of £562 minimum rental income per month required to meet lender criteria.

If we use the same principle but increase the property value to say £160K, at a 75% LTV mortgage this would give a debt of

£120K, so at the same interest rate of 6% APR this would mean we have a relative finance cost of £600 per month. Again, we multiply this cost by 150% to check against the lender criteria, and this provides a result of £900 per month minimum rental income required to fall inside lender policy. If the rental income was only £800 per month, the lender could reduce the amount loaned.

The reason I'm highlighting these things here is to make sure the point is laboured around whether funds are "gifted" or not. If they're gifted, there's no cost of finance to factor in for those funds, so your DSC calculations are unaffected. If they do attract any cost, this cost is factored into the lender calculations and ultimately this will reduce the amount you can borrow.

As a side note, at one stage back in 2023 (I think it was), due to the Bank of England base rate having increased from the once 0.10% in December 2021, up to its peak of that period of 5.25% from August 2023–July 2024, before it started coming back down again towards the end of 2024, lenders were coming to the market with a stress test rate of 100% - the lowest I've ever seen in my time. It's not even a stress test rate at all in this instance, really. This was a reflection of market conditions at the time though, and lenders wouldn't have been able to lend if they were stressing any higher.

Appreciating the base rate has been as high as 17% back in November of 1979 (well before my time), this period in 2023 – what I will loosely call a "base rate hike" – was combated by the lenders by offering competitive interest rates of around 6% APR, but with a staggering 7% arrangement fee, which allowed them to effectively charge the borrower a higher rate but only stress test against the 6% APR interest rate, which allowed them to continue to lend. We did some of these refinance deals ourselves at that time, and it's important to note that if you gear at 75% of the market value at the time, then add on the 7% arrangement fee, you've actually taken debt on that's more like 80% LTV (assuming you've added the arrangement fee to the loan, which is typical), so whenever the time comes to refinance again, you need to hope that the value has increased if you want to take out another 75% LTV loan, or you need to put cash in during the period before the refi, or you need to put cash in at the point of refi, to make sure you can get on to a new finance product at that time.

Inheritance:

Inherited funds are like gifted funds to a degree, but the gross funds received can be subject to tax – meaning the net funds received can sometimes be considerably lower. There's lots of variables to consider here, and the most important part of using inherited funds is the AML (Anti Money Laundering) and POSOF (Proof of Source of Funds) checks that the lawyers will do before they'll accept the funds for use in a property transaction.

It's really important to get all the relevant documentation in order, as there can sometimes be crazy requests. We had a client recently who was trying to use inherited funds – his dad had passed away six years ago. The lawyers from the lending bank were asking for a document to be signed from the deceased to confirm that the inheritor was actually authorised to use the funds! Now I've heard some crazy bastard requests from lawyers in my time, but I think this one takes the full packet of biscuits! I stay open-minded about the afterlife – I'm not a religious guy, but I am completely open minded about what might happen after we die. The fact is, we just don't know, so I remain optimistic there could be "something" after we pass on. But anyway, as far as I'm aware we are not in contact with the deceased, and I've never seen or heard of any dead person being resurrected to sign a document to allow a deal to go through. We did eventually convince them to see sense, and as always we got the deal over the line, which is always the most important thing!

REAL ESTATE WEALTH DEVELOPMENT : PROJECT F1

Sale of assets:

I've done this myself, multiple times over the years. My property journey actually started out way back in 2011-ish, when I bought a house across the road where I bought my first home to live in. The markets were still struggling due to the financial crash, and I made a cheeky offer on a two bed terraced that had been on the market for about 2 years. The house was valued at £115K, and I offered £80K. After initially being told to piss right off, about six months later the guy came and chapped my door and said they wanted to accept the offer! If only I'd known what I was doing back then, I could've cleaned up...

Unfortunately, I didn't know what I was doing, and I just saw property as a sound investment. Saved up cash, bought this one. Saved up more cash, bought another one. And repeated that process again. With some refinances being mixed in over a nine year period, I built my portfolio up to three units. Unbelievable. I literally could've refinanced the first property immediately and got all my cash out, then went on to offer on more properties, repeated that process, and I would've been a millionaire back in my twenties! Oh, if only I could turn back the time with my knowledge that I have now. I know so many people that did make a tonne of cash back then, and the biggest lesson that's taught me, is to start and start NOW on whatever goal it is you're going after.

Anyway... I owned these three properties for 10/11 years or so, then eventually came to sell them all on around 2023. I'd bought well and sold at a time when the market was decent, so extracted a good amount of cash from just these three units. At this point we were doing all that we are in REWD / REAL, so we ended up using that cash released from these properties to expand our home, with the Emandel Outhouse Project! The outhouse is my absolute home-based (Scotland-based) pride and joy, with the big bi-folding doors that open up in summertime, a covered outdoor kitchen area, the comfiest couch in the world, a gym, sauna, steam room, ice bath, as well as having various landscaped garden areas with BBQ and covered canopy areas for when it pisses down randomly on the hottest day of the year!

The sale of assets could've allowed us to go and continue to expand the portfolio, but ultimately we decided to improve our quality of life. Considering the success of the REAL Group operation and all that we have going on together there, it made sense for Emma and I to use our personal cash from the sale of these historical assets to improve our lifestyle. We'll never stop buying property deals – no question about that! And ultimately the point of this section of the finance strategy, is to make you realise that if you buy well, you will always make money somehow in this game. The longer you hold on to property, the more it increases in value – everybody knows this, and it's a proven repetitive situation since time began.

Now, we regularly buy and sell depending on the circumstances, both personally (in Emma's company, Chlodan) as well as throughout our different entities within the Group. Sell when it makes sense to do so, for whatever your reasons are.

Mezzanine funders:

Mezzanine finance (known as "Mezz") is more relative to development type projects, and this type of funding will typically sit behind your 1st Charge development funder, or even behind a 2nd Charge funder. Mezz allows you to access funding to complete the project that's maybe ran over in terms of budgeted cost projections – something that is very, very common in the development game!

Mezz funders will look at the GDV (gross development value) of the project, the saleability of the units and the scheme overall, to assess what level of funding they can get comfortable at for you. For example, if the GDV of the site is £10m, the development to date has cost £7m, but you now need another £1m to finish the project; mezz funders could look at this to provide you the £1m you need, at maybe a 25% APR rate, if they trust in the success of the project. It's high risk / high rate for this type of funding, so we've never actually used it on basic resi single unit deals. Due to the cost of finance, it always has to make sense from a viability perspective for you. If you take on funds for your project that just means the deal ends up costing you money, it's not a deal in the first place.

Mortgages:

More standard terminology on this one, and really a mortgage is known as any type of long term funding option, that most folk have on their homes. It's a common objective for people to want to pay off their mortgage – I think very, very differently, on the opposite end of the scale. For me, if I can borrow money that costs say 5% and I can use it to make say 10%+, then it's worth my while to take the money to continue building my wealth position. Mortgages, certainly against your main residential home, can be one of the cheapest ways to borrow money. (Not quite as cheap as 0% credit cards, right enough!)

When we talk about "exit funding", this is effectively a mortgage. At the moment, in the market, we are seeing Ltd. Co. lending rates around 6% APR at 75% LTVs, with various different incentives offered too, such as free surveys, free legals, cashback, and low arrangement fees. At the point of refinance, I like to lock in for five years, unless any reason to take a shorter-term view (i.e. lock in to only a two year deal), but in every case always on a fixed rate product, rather than a variable rate product.

Back in 2020 when we did our first portfolio deal, we borrowed around £7m of debt on a variable rate product at a bank margin of 4.3% above base rate. The base rate at the time was 0.25%, so upon drawdown it was all sunshine and rainbows! But then during the Covid-19 pandemic, over the next 2-3 years, we saw the base rate creep up steadily to 5.25%, giving a relative cost of finance of around 10% APR. We asked for support from the bank, who were offering 6.5% APR five year fixed-rate products to new clients. They refused, and wouldn't allow us to come off the products we had initially signed off on. We had even offered to pay them the £300K odds ETCs (Early Termination Charges) to move on to the new product! The answer was no.

Fortunately, since we had such a high yielding portfolio, we were able to battle it out over time, but it was probably the most challenging part of our whole business journey so far. As always, we figured it out! Not without our challenges.

Joint Venture partners:

As you will see from our corporate Group structure, if you refer back to previous pages, we scaled our operations massively by working with JV partners over the years. This type of combined effort can be a great way for people to get involved in property without actually being involved, as such. Most of our investment businesses are JV businesses, based around the simple model of our side putting in all the sweat equity by running the portfolio, managing all the admin, dealing with the agents and maintenance, as well as refurbishments. The JV partner side simply puts the money in and deals with some documentation signings as required for the likes of new acquisitions, refinances or sales.

Importantly, you need to remember that getting into business with someone is a big deal. A lot of people don't consider all the potential issues, and proceed to get into business with anyone that offers them some kind of opportunity. Business is highly complex – difficult situations will arise from nowhere and put you to the ultimate test, time and time again. Think about the necessary documentation required such as Shareholders'

Agreement, Articles of Association, and any loan documentation for money involved.

Everyone involved in the business will have to sign up to the likes of Personal Guarantees (known as PGs). There will be calls and meetings required for ILA (which stands for independent legal advice), around the signing of the PGs. Documentation signings in the most part are required to be wet ink versions – meaning scanned copies aren't good enough. It does still baffle me that in 2025, when we're about to colonise the planet Mars, that we can't have a digital legal and land registry system – but I'm confident we can't be too far away from it now!

Anyone you get into business with should have a minimum level of experience, and this will dictate their expectations of the venture. We've found that inexperienced people can cause a lot of undue problems and stress, simply because they don't truly understand what's going on. It seems to be the case, particularly in the property space, that anyone will get into business with anyone, without actually discussing things in any great detail first, to establish whether skillsets are complimentary or otherwise.

We've learned the hard way a few times over the years. All I'm saying is, don't get into business with just anyone. It can be great too, though... I'm very lucky that Alex, Conar and I all get on, are similarly minded, and yet bring three very different perspectives to the table. This balanced view is what creates a challenging yet sensible discussion which allows us, most of the time anyway, to come up with something that pushes us forward in the right direction.

Crowd funding:

Crowd funding is more typically used on development projects rather than investment projects. It can get quite messy from a security perspective when trying to crowd fund a residential buy to let portfolio, for example, that has 50 units in it, plus bank funding. We explored this type of funding a few times but never managed to get it off the ground, even when we had large scale developments on the go that could've lent themselves to it. It seems to be more popular down in England, but not so common for us up in Scotland – in my experience, anyway.

The principle of crowd funding involves multiple people contributing a smaller value to the pot, which creates a big pot, and that larger pot is then used to fund a project of some kind. If you've never checked it out, type in "crowd funding for property" into your search engine of choice – you will see there's tonnes to choose from. I know a few guys that have loaned funds to a platform and been paid around 5-10% APR. I also know others who have borrowed from a platform and paid costs similar to bridging products, including arrangement fees, monthly chargeable interest (sometimes retained), exit fees, survey & QS costs, and various other fees depending on the situation of the project. It's not necessarily the cheapest solution of funding, but it can be practical and flexible depending on what you're looking to do.

Vendor finance:

Simply put, vendor finance is when the seller funds your purchase! Now, you might be thinking why anyone would ever consider this when usually the whole purpose of selling the property is to get it off their plate and cash in on any equity – and yes, nine times out of ten that is the case. However, if you can imagine a situation where a seller has an unencumbered asset (meaning they have no debt secured against it), and they are in a position where they don't need any money now, they could sell you their property, and take a charge against it for the value of the sale, which would give them legal right to resell the property if you were to breach the agreement of the loan.

Vendor finance is a great strategy, and it's one that's used in wider business scenarios too, not specific to property. Charges don't need to be 1st tier either; it's by negotiation and agreement, so you could still use mainstream bank funding with a 1st Charge and have a vendor take a 2nd Charge, allowing you to have your deals fully funded. If you think about a situation where the owner of a business is looking to sell, they might be happy that you are taking all the liabilities off their hands, and they could take their payout over a 1/2/5/10 year period. Getting creative on finance is my favourite part of business – there are always solutions to be put on the table that most folk maybe aren't thinking about. Most important thing is to suss out your vendor and find what they want out of the deal being done, to establish whether or not they could be a potential funding solution to minimise the cash you are required to put in yourself.

Government grants:

The government is constantly issuing grants to support business growth and development. It changes depending on where they want to see improvements. Back in the day when we had a building company, we took on I think six or seven apprentices – young guys straight out of school, supporting the other more experienced tradesmen such as joiners, plumbers, painters, electricians, etc. It was around £5K per apprentice that we received, for creating employment and giving people an opportunity to get into work. I must stress that unfortunately, that in the most part these young guys were not interested to work or learn – they really just wanted to piss about on their phones all day and do as little work as they possibly could, as they were still getting paid at the end of the day regardless. This is true of the majority of tradesmen we've encountered, to be fair, regardless of whether they are an apprentice! Now, though, we do have a great network of subcontractors all over Scotland – using subcontractors seems to be a much better way to operate, since they will turn up at the day and time they said they would, they do a good job because they want to get paid, they want more work from us as we have constant demand, and they are generally much more reliable that having a staff tradesman onboard.

If I've not said it yet, I'll say it now – please don't start a building company unless you are the guy on the tools, managing the tradesmen and the projects. Being involved in that game was one of the worst times of my whole life! Subbies all the way! Anyway, tradesmen rant over...

We have around 20 staff at the time of writing this book, and we've had various types of grant funding for bringing people into work. Each Council seems to have their varying degrees of terms for grants, but we've found some consistency with Falkirk Council, offering us 50% of the salary as a Grant, for the first six months of employment. This type of funding can really help with your expansion plans, as it gives you a bit of a breather to support cashflow as you look to grow.

Between the apprentices and office staff, we must have received over £50K in Grant funding. It's always a good idea to tie in with your local Business Gateway – they're usually pretty well versed in what's on offer.

Your own liquidity / savings:

So, if you have your own liquidity, including savings, why would you not want to put this to use in your property venture? Well, it's always good to have a buffer for when things don't work out as planned, and in our view this is where your own personal cash could be brought into play. I'm sure you can see by now that there's tonnes of different ways to fund your property business, so you don't need to use your own cash, and actually it's always strange to me that a lot of people will *only* use their own cash, which massively holds them back.

If you think about it, if you have your own pot of cash of say £100K, many would consider this a decent chunk of cash to get started out, and indeed it is. On average, there's around 35K of cash required as a minimum, so by the time you buy two units – you might be lucky to get three – that cash is now tied up until you refinance, assuming you're building a buy to let business rather than flipping units. In reality, you might end up doing a bit of both.

So, say you've done three deals, and they're all buy to let, so you're now refinancing them. If you leave £10K in every deal, you've maybe recycled say £70K of the £100K cash, so you're ready to crack on now and buy another two units. If they are on the same basis, then you will buy the two, refinance them, and the cash pot would reduce down to £50K. You do one more deal, then maybe one other after that, so call it seven units in the portfolio from the £100K cash pot, noting that you would still have some extra cash in the bank at that point too, in this example, so you might get to eight units then.

Now, that's all well and good, but you've just proved to yourself that the system works, you know what you're doing, you're more experienced... but you've drained your cash pot. At this stage, if you're not willing to go out and raise more funds, you will halt your progress. So the question for me is, how big do you really want to grow your property business? If you're content with a small portfolio of ten units, producing you around £2K a month of income, allowing a bit of bleed for voids, arrears and maintenance costs, then that's all good. BUT, really, when you know what you're doing in this game, I really don't understand why you would ever want to stop buying deals.

The takeaway here should just be to realise that even though you might have what most would consider a decent starting pot, it can deplete quite quickly. Obviously in the above examples, too, it's very much based on buying deals with the minimum amount of cash each time. In reality, the cash requirements per deal vary significantly.

Overdrafts:

Overdrafts are an expensive form of funding and banks generally don't like to provide them to property related businesses, whether investment or trading. That said, it doesn't have to be a business overdraft; you could have a personal overdraft and dip into those funds, if required. We have had an overdraft in the past, but don't use them anymore. The time we did have it in place, though, we used the £5K-odds – right at the start of our journey, to get us out a couple of holes! Nothing serious, just cashflow management, but it was quick and easy access and allowed us to solve problems with ease, albeit with a 40% odds APR finance cost attached. We only ever used it for 7-10 days or so when we needed to, and so the cost was relative and perfectly manageable in these cases.

Generally, the question comes up all the time from clients, should they be looking to take out credit (whether credit cards, bank loans, overdrafts etc.) in the company name or their personal names. It's an easy response – personal name every time. The reasons for that are 1) you will always get much better deals from taking personal debt and 2) it's unlikely the banks will offer your company any options anyway, especially at the start of your operation when it's a newco.

Challenger banks:

We've seen such a massive shift in the lending market since we got started out back in 2018 / 2019. Really it's just a terminology thing – they are simply banks that lend to limited companies for property businesses. I'll rhyme a few off here as examples, but note this market is constantly changing, and certainly for the better in more recent times:

- TMW – The Mortgage Works

- TML – The Mortgage Lender

- FHL – Foundation Home Loans

- Aldermore

- Shawbrook

- Together Money

- Lendinvest

- Paragon

- Kensington

- Precise

- West One

- Redwood

Really, when Alex and I started out, there were only one or two lenders for buy to let to limited companies in Scotland. Then when we added in that we liked the lower value, high-yielding properties, that just basically eliminated us from any lenders that did exist. This has been such an interesting part of the journey for me – we are now so well-versed with these lenders, their terms, what they like and what they don't, and who's good to deal with and who's not, and why.

Everybody wants to buy a property at a discount, and then – the day they conclude – refinance it to a different lender to create a "day 1 refinance"! And whilst it *can* be done, as always it is subject to the deal specifics as to whether or not it can be done. One question that comes up continually is whether or not this is legal. I can assure you there are no legislative restraints around this strategy and we, and our clients, are repeating this process on a daily basis. There is some confusion around the CML – the Council of Mortgage Lenders – where some people incorrectly understood that "the six month rule" was a rule. There are no

January 2020

Annual Objective:

Own 300 properties by end of year.

March 2020

Coronavirus hits!

That's the end of that then...!

September 2020

Well well well...

Watch this space.

REWD Group

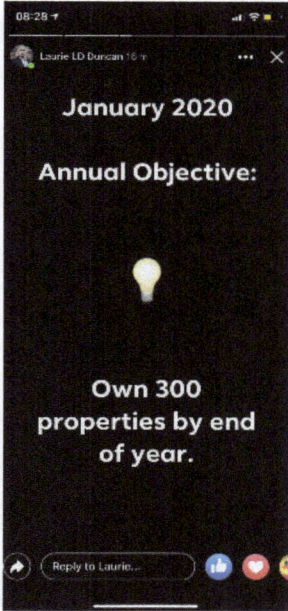

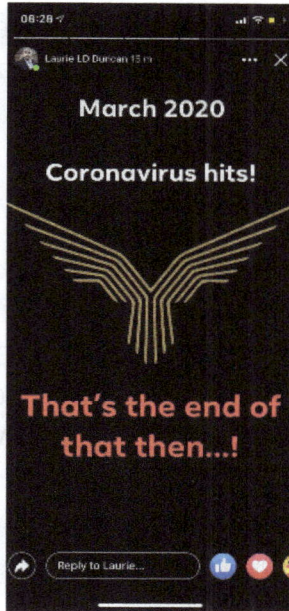

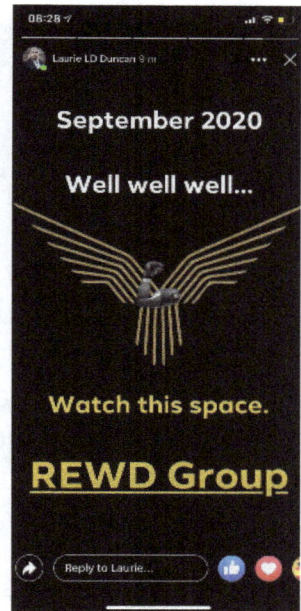

rules, only guidance, and it's up to the banks themselves to decide if they want to adhere to any guidelines. So, there is no six month rule, there is no restriction on day 1 refinances, only the lenders themselves.

Again, this market is constantly shifting, but at the time of writing, the following lenders will entertain day 1 refinances:

- FHL (min £75K property value)

- Paragon (min £75K property value)

- Lendinvest (min £75K property value)

- Aldermore (min £50K property value)

- Together

- Shawbrook

Challenger banks, we salute you! Keep on challenging and bringing us more and more competitive products, please!

Private Investors

Think of these guys as the people who have the ability to fund your financial freedom. They are so important, they've got their own section in the book (I nearly said little section, but it will not be small)! This chapter will probably grow arms and legs as I think and write about all the creativity we've had with private money loaned to our business. Genuinely, I cannot stress enough how big a deal private investors can be in this property game.

We have investors ranging from £20K to £500K, and multiples of them too. We have unsecured loans, we have personally guaranteed loans, we have 1st Charge Secured loans, we have loans secured by PCGs (Parent Company Guarantee), and we have loans secured against shares. Some people view this as "pooled investment", when actually it's a completely different concept – we're not pulling together funds to do any specific project of any kind, we're simply set up to take in private money to support our cashflow of all Group operations, and in return we pay an interest on that loan to the lender. All businesses need funding of some kind, so we can either borrow from the banks or we can borrow from individuals or corporate lenders. If we can create a scenario, like we have, where the lenders believe in us and our business activities, and they are happy to receive an interest payment in exchange for funds loaned, then what's the difference between private funding and bank funding?

I mentioned RR1 earlier, REWD Resi 1 Limited – refer back to our corporate structure chart if you need to. We called this type of company within the Group structure a "Feeder Company". The reason we set this up, very much back in the day, was to give a clear protection to private investor securities, to avoid having them mixed up in the wider portfolio where we had commercial term loans with bank securities of a Bond & Floating Charge (BFC). A BFC is known as a Debenture in English law – same thing, different terminologies, that gives the bank security over all company assets, including cash, stock, vehicles, IT, and anything else it owns.

We don't really have a requirement for a Feeder Company these days, since we rarely have an investor looking for a 1st Charge Security on a single unit. When we started out though, this was how we handled the majority of private loans. Now, after years of being in business, we have an established brand, with reputation and credibility, so most people prefer to lend unsecured in exchange for a higher rate of interest paid. Starting out, offering a 1st Charge is a great way to answer the question of "why would anyone give ME their money?!" Well, why not? Do you believe in yourself? Do you have a quality deal that provides suitable security? Does the private investor – a family friend, a work colleague, a family member, a friend of a friend, a random person from a networking event – do they have some cash in the bank and are looking for a safe solid return on their investment? If so, you can facilitate that, by bringing all your knowledge and experience together, and making a proposal to them.

Let me give you an example, and I'll get even more creative here for you to labour this point, and it is in fact a REAL example of a deal we did back around 2019...

35 Dryburgh Avenue in Denny. It's a three bed flat, ex-Council property, and would rent for a minimum of £600 per

month. The property is on the open market for £65K. The home report is £65K too. We arranged a viewing, liked what we saw; there was maybe a £5K refurb to do, but that was all. Property was generally in good nick. Always looking for a good deal, we (very cheekily!) offered £40K, making the point about the applicable ADS, inflating the refurb projections, and most importantly, positioning ourselves as a cash buyer that could conclude in a matter of weeks. I must note here, at the point we were offering, we didn't know how we would fund the purchase, as we didn't have the cash to buy it, but we certainly believed that we could find it, so we negotiated with confidence!

One thing you should always, always, ALWAYS do when you're at viewings or speaking to the seller, is understand their situation. When you know what's driving them, you can use this to your advantage. If you don't understand the seller situations, you are pissing in the wind, my friend. This seller's situation was an inheritance case. She was the only person involved – there were no other family members to consult, meaning she was the sole decision maker. The property was unencumbered (meaning there was no debt to be repaid from the sale), so to the seller, the thought of having £40K net received to her bank account in only a few weeks would create a life-changing situation. I can't remember if they initially told us to piss off – sellers usually do with the first offer – but anyway, we held our ground, she accepted, and we pushed the deal into legals. Remember, this deal was on the open market – anyone could've agreed this one.

The interesting and creative bit then came after the purchase was agreed. Like I said, we didn't have the money to buy it, so we now had to find it. We'd become well accustomed to this process by now, as we'd built the portfolio up to around 40 units I think when we did the Dryburgh deal. Anyway, in true REAL style, we put the deal in front of an investor we knew had some cash in the bank. We requested £50K from them, in exchange for a 1st Charge Security – remember, the property had a home report of £65K, so their £50K against the £65K meant they were funding at a 77% loan to value ratio: a solid security in anyone's book! What this meant for us was that we were now fully funded in the deal. This investor, since we were buying at £40K, had now funded the ADS tax, our legal fees AND the refurb. Not only that, there was STILL extra cash in our bank account to support with general cashflow.

We are happy, the seller is happy, the investor is happy – what's not to like about this equation?

CASH LEFT IN = £0!

CASHFLOW (AFTER REFI!) = £425PCM!

So, we acquired, we refurbed, we let the property out at £650 per month (so that was an extra 50 quid more than we thought we were going to get on the rent), and we then refinanced... at an end value of £75K. So, 75% of £75K = £56K new mortgage value, which repaid the investor their 50K, plus their interest due. I can't remember the interest value, but call it 6% APR, and we probably paid a full 12 months' interest even if we only used the cash for 6 months – we did these types of deals all the time at the start, to incentivise private funders to work with us. £75K – £56K = £19K equity created on this deal now, after refinance, with a net cashflow (before voids, arrears and maintenance) of

300 per month. I really, really hope you can see how the combination of buying property at a discount, using private money, and application of the BRRR strategy, can completely transform your life – you don't need to repeat this process too often to quit your job and focus full time on property. We put no money into this deal – it was fully funded, and it was on the open market.

Before we'd ever worked with any private funders, I always had this weird image in my head of a big boardroom of really wealthy business owners, sitting round a big, old wooden table, smoking cigars, wearing pinstripe suits, with top hats and canes. For whatever reason, this is how I imagined pitching for private investment. What might completely blow your mind is the fact that there is private money EVERYWHERE. So many people are just sitting on cash in their banks, looking for something to do with it. We got our best results simply from speaking to everyone we knew about what we were doing – I think it's fair to say that there wasn't anyone that wasn't interested. We were maybe in our mid-thirties when we got kicked off, and there weren't many other people going out there and starting up in business, certainly not so many in property, and we found that people like bricks and mortar as security and they tend to understand the strategy easier than the likes of stocks and shares, where I think most folk just take a bit of a punt. Explaining to people what we did, how it worked, combined with a bit of our natural charisma, really served us well. These private investors are all people we know, or have gotten to know, and they are just anyone with some money in the bank, looking to earn a return off it. There's no hoity toity, no pitch decks, no pin stripe suits, top hats or canes. I guarantee you that if you continue to talk and tell people about you and your business, and explain the offering you can provide to them for little to no involvement, you will find people that want to listen, and you will find private investment.

The example above was a secured example, but I mentioned earlier that nowadays most people lend to us on an unsecured basis. This is where shit starts to get properly REAL. Imagine a scenario where you take in £100K of private investment, unsecured. You are now able to combine this with highly leveraged bridging finance, geared typically around 85% loan to purchase price (LTPP). If you buy a property for £50K, you would need a rough breakdown of cash as follows:

- 15% deposit cash (based on 85% LTPP) = £7.5K

- 8% ADS (at time of writing) = £4K

- Legals budget = £1.5K

- Source fee = £6K

- Assume it's a tenanted property so 1) it's bringing in rent from day 1, and 2) there's no refurb required

So, 7.5K+4K+1.5K+6K = only £19K of cash required to do this deal. In theory, with £100K of cash unsecured from this private investor, you can do five of these deals, and still have £5K of cash left in the bank.

Say the end value is £80K. When you refinance, you take out a new debt of 75% of £80K = £60K. You then need to clear off your original debt of 85% of £50K = £42K, meaning this deal has only left in around £5 grand of cash after refinance costs. I have always maintained that if I can buy a property for £10 grand (or less) every time, I will be a happy man! When you're leaving £10K in a deal, you're always getting that cash back within 3–4 years anyway, so I am completely relaxed about that. If you're always raising more funds and you're always doing more deals, your property business will continue to grow.

We have various different styles of deal calculators that will automatically produce data to support you analysing the information presented. For anyone interested in a copy of that, if you head over to **www.thepropertyuniversity.co.uk**, we'll happily send them over to you. One thing to make sure you don't get caught up on though, is whatever the data says in the calculator being considered gospel. You will never know the true success of a deal until you have exited it. By exiting, I mean either refinanced it or sold it off. If you are refinancing, the one thing that makes or breaks a deal is the end value provided by the surveyor on behalf of the bank. If, in the end, that value is as you expected it to be, then great. If it's £10K less, you have a decision to make as to whether you accept it or not. If it's a £10K up-val (increased value from expectation) then you're off to the races and have collected some tax-free money in the form of a bank loan! There will be good deals and there will be bad deals – as long as you buy right and keep applying the strategy, you will get to where you want to be. If a deal really goes south, sell it, recoup, and move on to the next one. Buying right is absolutely fundamental in this game, so make sure you're buying decent deals from reputable sourcing agents. The amount of times we see and hear about "dodgy deals" getting presented, and bought, is frightening. So, so many people out there are out to shaft you – be careful who you choose to listen to.

Importantly in all of the private investor finance side, you can't just take cash in willy-nilly without checking where it came from – you have obligations under AML (Anti-Money Laundering) legislation. You need to verify IDs of the people you are working with, which typically is in the form of a passport (for ID), a driver licence (for ID and address verification), and a utility bill (but not a mobile phone bill) dated within the last three months. You also need to verify the Source of Funds (SOF) – the lawyers will not use any funds until they are completely satisfied that both AML and SOF has been successfully complied with. I've seen this time and time again, where people do not give respect to the requirements of AML, and ultimately if these checks haven't been done, deals can fall down due to delays on the buyer side. It's always a good idea to have your funds approved well in advance of settlement.

Private investor funding, at the start of our journey, was always on a secured basis. It took around 18 months to 2 years of doing regular deals, using private funds, paying back at refinance, and just repeating this process over and over again, working with various different people and, I guess, 1) proving the strategy, to ourselves and the investors! and 2) demonstrating our credibility and building up that reputation over time.

Secured loans are very easy to track – you basically don't even need to track these. The refinance stage always takes care of repaying the private investor back, and it's dealt with by the lawyers automatically. Folk always ask the question of: "But what if I don't get all my money back out of the deal!?" Well, you might not! That's all part of the refinance game – dodgy valuations WILL happen, as will up-vals! So ride the wave,

continue doing deals, and you will get to where you want to be. Even if there is a bit of cash left in the deal, it doesn't have to be your investors' money. The savvy among us will go back to the section on credit cards and realise that if you have left any cash in the deal, you can have that financed at 0% APR and repaid over a longer period of time using your cashflow from your rental income.

Unsecured loans on the other hand, must, must, must be tracked. We found that after a bit of trust was built up with the investors, they were more interested to go unsecured as we would pay a higher rate of interest – higher risk, higher return. No more visits to lawyers to sign paperwork, no more waiting around for the deal to conclude before they started earning interest, no more analysis of a particular security before they would loan – they just loaned funds, they were earning money immediately; very simple paperwork done front end, no more paperwork, then we would just crack on doing our thing, using these loaned funds to support the cashflow of our general Group operations.

Now there's pros and cons of using unsecured funding, but for us, it was an absolute game-changer. We were now in a position where we could use private investor funds, combined with bridging finance at 85% LTPP (loan to purchase price), meaning every single time we did a property deal, we were funded with 100% of all costs. We could use these funds for paying the likes of sourcing fees or legal fees, for refurbs, or to increase our marketing budget to create more deal flow, to increase our staff base, to cover any shortages of dodgy vals – literally to cover costs of whatever element of our business we required. So at this point, I reiterate, it is absolutely essential to track unsecured private investor funding – it's no different to having multiple bank loans, with different durations of loan, different interest rates relative to timescales, different repayment dates, different use locations throughout the Group – you get the picture. Again, we are very lucky to have Mr Alex Robertson, who tracks all this data and keeps us right as to what has been allocated to where and when, for what reason, then when it's due to be paid back too. This task is absolutely fundamental to your business growth – I'm sure you can appreciate that depending on how much funding you take on, this can become quite the project. It certainly did for us!

I think at our peak we maybe had around £5m of private investor funding in play, allocated to different aspects of Group activity. At this stage of our journey we are in the process of repaying all of that debt down – we don't need these sums in the Group anymore, and we don't want to continue paying the interest costs either. Thankfully we have multiple successful Group companies, all growing at a steady pace, so we are in a transition mode now to get into the position of only using our own cash, although it's always nice to know that if we did need to go out and raise some flexible private funding, we've proved to ourselves that all that cash is out there, as well as proving that we are capable to achieve raising these levels of funds.

Brokers

Ahhh, brokers...! These guys come in so many different shapes and sizes. And I must be honest, I don't really rate brokers, generally speaking. If your finance broker is also a property investor, doing their own deals, different types of deals and at varying value levels, knows all the lenders and their criteria, then okay – I think there is value in a broker of that sort. Note, though, they are few and far between! Perhaps obviously, they will always, always, always, tell you everything you want to hear.

They will tell you that you can get whatever it is that you desire, and they will believe that you can too – even if you cannot. They will over-promise you the earth and deliver zero in return for your wasted time, and potentially even an upfront fee of some kind. I have honestly lost count of the number of brokers we have been through over the years – every time, every new broker, tells us they are the key to unlock some new type of funding, or a new lender, or a new creative solution. Most of the time, it's a complete waste of time, so now we don't even engage with anyone else other than those we use on a regular basis. I've found that having a bit of pull in the decision making processes has been valuable to us, to get deals done when others would've thought they might not have been possible.

Most brokers want to get you into something that's nice and easy – they do not necessarily care about you or your business. They just want paid quickly and for doing the minimal amount of work. There's a bit of me that respects the "minimal effort, maximum return" thing, but the number of times I've been told by brokers that something isn't possible, then I go and do the digging myself to find out that it *is* in fact possible, is genuinely unreal. The thing is that brokers (assuming they are not professional property investors) do not think about property deals they way you will think about deals. They don't think about creativity they way I do, that's for sure. Very often, the responses are very much like "computer says no"!

There are companies out there that will offer you a finance brokerage service without any front-end fees (i.e. fees charged to you as the borrower) – they make their money from the lenders paying them introducer fees (known as back-end fees), so they don't charge the borrower. Of course, I've tried these services in the past too, but again they are a complete waste of time. If you're just looking to refinance your home mortgage or do some kind of simple finance deal, then fine; it might work out and be a bit cheaper than using a broker, but if you're serious about becoming a professional property investor, you need to work with someone that will work with you to achieve the results you are able to. Don't let your property journey be impacted by brokers that do not understand "the game".

Most brokers are analysing lender options from the total market, but not all. If you're working with someone that only uses certain lenders for whatever reason – it could be that they prefer some lenders as they are paid higher commissions from them, or maybe they are part of a brokerage group that only has access to some banks but not others – this could also limit your growth.

I've found that in most cases I tend to know more about finance solutions than the brokers do. Note I call them "finance solutions" rather than "mortgages", because thinking outside the box is what's going to create solutions instead of barriers. No broker is going to put you in touch with a private investor that would come in to fund 100% LTV against what might be considered an unmortgageable property from some lenders, since that's outside of their criteria. So don't be restricted by what brokers might tell you – there is always a solution to your finance needs. You just need to think creatively.

Acquisition V Exit

We've talked about Term Loans, and we've talked about Bridging. Really, these terminologies are relative to Acquisition funding and Exit funding, respectively. Bridging is short-term funding. Term Loans or mortgages (just different terminologies for the same thing) are longer-term funding solutions. Bridging is more expensive, generally roughly double the interest rate of a term loan product.

Of course, a broker will tell you they can get you cheaper rates...

At the point of acquisition, we want to have a kind of funding that is fast and flexible. This is bridging finance. Ideally, we don't want a physical survey of the property, as I'm sure you will appreciate that this could spook the seller in an already-distressed situation. Not only that, but surveys can add time to the transaction settlement – as well as cost for you, the buyer. Most of the time, the lenders we work with will accept what is called a desktop survey, where they analyse data from an online database and take comfort from the expected value of the property, and they will fund against that at around 80% LTPP. Sellers just want to know their property will be sold, quickly, in exchange for a discounted price, and anything outside of that simple process gives them cause for concern.

We've already covered the LTVs, rates, and other costs in bridging finance, as well as the process involved, so please refer back to that section if you need to go over that again. We do have a lot of online content in the property university that covers this type of stuff in great detail too, so check that out if you want a more in depth education on the specifics of this type of finance. Learn bridging – work with it. It will be absolutely key to your success. If you don't use bridging finance, it will seriously hamper your growth.

After we've acquired the property, we then want to get it off the bridge ASAP, since it is expensive finance compared to a term loan. Assuming you're keeping it to let it out in some way, you want to refurb it (if it does in fact need a refurb), then once it's looking all nice and shiny, get the surveyor out to provide the valuation that will be passed to the bank for lending.

A few points here, then...

Firstly, you want to get in and out of the bridge ASAP. My record is six weeks from the date of acquisition to the date of cash landing back in the bank account. Obviously in this case there wasn't any refurb to do – it was what you might call a straight finance flip, from the purchase price to the actual value. So if you buy something for £100K, and it's actually worth £150K, you can immediately refinance to the value of 75% of the £150K, which means you will near enough recycle all your cash depending on what other costs are involved in the transaction.

Secondly, as soon as you possibly can, you want to get the surveyor out to value the property for the term loan funder. That is always after the refurb is complete, if there is a refurb. Don't send the valuer out when the property is in a complete mess, as they will most likely down-value it. Most of the time you can obtain a free valuation as an incentive from the lender. This is an absolutely sensational feature of term loans, as you can have the property valued at no cost to you, apart from a little time I guess, before you take the decision to proceed or otherwise. Remember, too, that you don't need to accept the valuation if you don't like it – you could have three lenders all offering you a free valuation, so you could get them all done, then pick your favourite one!

Thirdly, the property does not need to be occupied when you make the move to term loan funding. We talked about DSC earlier – if the property is empty at the time of your refinance, this does not mean the lender will not lend. You just need to provide the expected rental income and the lender will assess the loan on that basis. I actually prefer, as part of standard process, to deal with the refinance first before putting a tenant in. When there is an existing tenant, access becomes difficult, as they need to

commit time to allow the surveyor in, and the condition the property is in when someone is living in it is not always the nicest environment – we are all different animals!

During the refinance process, you will increase your debt value but lower the interest rate. Note any monthly % rate quoted should just be multiplied by 12 to calculate the APR (ie. 1% per month = 12% APR). Here is an example of a property purchased for £70K that has a value of £100K:

- Acquisition:

    o £70K purchase price

    o 85% LTPP loan = 85% * 70K = £59.5K

    o Finance cost = 59.5K * 12% APR / 12 months = £595 per month

- Exit:

    o £100K end value

    o 75% LTV loan = 75% * 100K = £75K

    o Finance cost = 75K * 6% APR / 12 months = £375 per month

So in this example, the debt was £59.5K at a cost of £595 per month on the bridge, with a rate of 1% per month (or 12% APR). At refinance we increased the debt to £75K, but since the cost of finance was now 6% APR, the relative cost reduces to £375 per month.

It's common not to make any money on a deal until you refinance. This is a long-term game – if you're in the property space to go after the "get rich quick" thing then you're playing the wrong game. Don't wait to buy property – buy property and wait.

Rates, LTVs & Securities

At the time of writing this, in early 2025 (after loosely starting to write the book in 2023 then telling myself lots of excuses as to why I didn't complete it), it is very typical for lenders to offer a 75% LTV (loan to value) at a term loan interest rate, anywhere from 4.5% APR but averaging around 6% APR, certainly for Limited Company lending. Security-wise, they will always take 1st Charge and a PG.

A Personal Guarantee (PG) is a type of security that exists across the majority of lending options these days, it seems. I don't think I've ever worked with any type of institutional lending where there has not been a requirement of a PG from the lender. Our residential buy to let portfolio is currently valued around £25m, meaning our PGs must total around £20m. PGs are very simple – sign the documents, and the bank will give you the money. If you don't sign the documents, you won't get the money. So ask yourself: do you want the money?

The Rates, LTVs & Securities do vary by lender, but in the most part they are broadly similar. Lenders need to be competitive, otherwise they won't lend out any money since nobody would want to borrow from them. The lending landscape is a really interesting one to me − it is constantly evolving. Any time new lenders come into play, and there's been two in Scotland already since the start of 2025, it keeps all the other existing lenders on their toes knowing they need to keep that pencil sharp and service level up, if they are going to retain their market position. The incentives are what I've noticed improve the most over the last couple of years − free surveys, free legals, and cashback all spring to mind. With the base rate now seemingly on a downward trend, I'm hoping we continue to see the lender rates come down a little bit more too, to an ideal relative 5% APR − this would make me happy!

One really important point about lenders and their offerings is to consider what type of product you choose. At this stage of the journey, for me, I like to lock into a five year deal on a fixed rate of interest at the point of refinance, then sit back and let the portfolio do its thing. This might seem like an obvious statement, but this type of deal wasn't always available. During our main period of growth, which was in 2020 and during the Covid-19 pandemic, we pushed all the properties on to commercial loans with the one lender and all on the same product, which was a five year deal with a variable interest rate of around 4.5% above the base rate. This was fine when the base rate was at its low of 0.25%, but as the rate crept up we incurred massive hikes in finance costs and it was ultimately the variability that caused us major grief in a lot of different ways. I've always liked knowing set values, so I know what's coming in every month and I know what's going out − I didn't want any variability. At the time, though, this was the only option for us that allowed us to gear aggressively and grow the portfolio, so we signed up to the product and started to ride that wave.

Man, to think about all that's gone on since back in 2020 – if we had been able to sign up to a fixed rate of say 7% APR, that would've been a game-changer for us. That said, the journey just wouldn't be the journey if it wasn't for all that's gone on, so I remain full of gratitude for all the learnings and experiences, as it is without any doubt what's made us who we are today. There's lots of situations like that for everyone as we go through this crazy thing called life, but I always try my best not to regret anything we've done. I do often reflect on our vast experiences and like to laugh at them now, in terms of just how stupid or crazy or out-there or wild – or whatever else you want to call it – some of our ideas have actually been!

I'll finish this section with a bit of advice:

- F　　Follow

- O　　One

- C　　Course

- U　　Until

- S　　Successful

Please don't try to take on the world like we did! OK, we survived to tell the tale, but it's so clear to me now to see why the majority of businesses fail within their first 3 years. So, so, so many learnings, but – like I say – I am grateful for them all now. Stick to the things that work, like building a buy to let portfolio, and FOCUS on that until you're at a point where you genuinely do not have to work ever again, if you choose.

A Bond and Floating Charge (or a BFC) can be another common security requirement for some lenders, more so at acquisition stage rather than exit stage, but I'll cover this a bit further on in the Legals section. In England, this is referred to as a Debenture, so just be aware of these different terminologies if they are to arise.

Buying Portfolios

Portfolio acquisitions changed everything for us. Not only did it put us on a bit of a pedestal in the property scene, but these types of deals gave us so much experience. At the time, there weren't so many people doing these larger types of deals, so we did stand out a bit by pushing ourselves into this realm. The first portfolio deal we ever did was 82 units across Lanarkshire back in 2020, again during the Covid-19 pandemic, with an AMV (aggregate market value) of £3.7m, and we purchased it for £2.9m − so around a 20% discount. We funded the purchase with a commercial loan at 90% LTPP, which we were able to obtain since we had a 20% discount against the true values of the units, meaning there was only around 10% of cash that had to go into the deal as deposit contribution, then around £250K of additional acquisition costs. All that totalled up to around £500K-odds of cash required in total to do the deal. This was our first portfolio acquisition, and it was our first three JVs (joint ventures) − a bold move in anyone's book! But it pushed us and our JV partners on into the major leagues of the property world.

That deal was "too big" for any one person we were involved with at the time, so we had to split it up into three packages to allow both us and our JV partners to take it on. It's funny to think back on this one now, as it was such a beautifully-structured acquisition, and for the first year or two things were going really well. Unfortunately, as is life, the sunshine and rainbows never lasted, and we started to encounter problems as the base rate started to increase. Ultimately, we got to the point where any cashflow was being eaten up by the finance costs, and it was becoming unsustainable. We agreed a deal with all three JV partners that Alex and I would take full control over the companies, remove the JV partners' liabilities to the commercial loans, and this would be in exchange for commitment to repay their DLAs (Directors' Loan Accounts) back to them over an agreed period of extended time. Business deals don't always work out – I've learned that the hard way now multiple times – but this scenario was all amicable, I'm pleased to say, and we all went our separate ways with that plan in place.

After the first portfolio deal had concluded, and we announced our achievement to the social media masses, we saw an influx of opportunities land in our inbox. I vividly remember a point in early 2021 as we sat in our office at the time, which was in a building called Temperance House on Falkirk High Street. Now, this place was not much of an office; it was actually an old multi-use building we took on as one of our many commercial to residential conversion (also known as "C2R"!) projects around 2019-2022. That office space is now what is known as "Flat 5, Temperance House", and it's the only one unit that we sold out of the six flats that we developed in that building – we kept the other five to hold in one of our Group portfolios. I've not gone into too much detail around the C2R developments we did, but there were a few. The developments game is way more complex than the off-market resi trading game, so I am absolutely delighted to not be involved in that anymore! Our C2R projects probably merit their own book – maybe that will be book 3 then! (Watch this space...) Anyway, in this room of Temperance House, Alex and I sat there on a cold, wet, winter's morning as the emails came flooding in, with various different portfolios for sale. It was like we just opened a door to Narnia, and we could see monumental opportunities in front of us, now that we'd stepped into portfolio deal territory. It was unbelievable. We bid on maybe 20-odd portfolios within the first 2-3 months of 2021. We met loads of people that wanted to do these types of deals too. We could see a path ahead of us now where, if we just kept growing and growing in this space, we would get to where we wanted to be.

Unfortunately for us, this was around the same time we decided to start:

- REWD Developments Limited (known as "REWD DEV"), for commercial projects and land developments

- REWD Building Co Limited (known as "BCL"), a building company with all our own tradesmen

- REWD Training Limited (now REAL Property Scotland Limited, or "RPS"), what was going to be our property education company but has morphed into a one-stop-shop style deal machine, now supporting hundreds of clients build their own property businesses

So, DEV and BCL were absolute shit-shows. I say that, but actually we do still have DEV and these days we use it for residential flips, either flipping through auction as an immediate flip, or if we take on units to refurb to sell to open market homebuyers. BCL, without doubt, was a total fucking shitshow. You might wonder why I'm talking about this stuff at the Portfolios section of the book and, well, it's really to get the point across that if we had not pissed about with these companies that caused us so much aggro, and if we'd just focused on buying single resi units, doing portfolio deals, and simply building the buy to let business, we would very likely be much further on! Okay, I know we still have 300+ units so it's a solid result, but these trading companies took our eye off the buy to let ball, and whilst we learnt tonnes of very valuable lessons from them at an early stage of our journey (and yes, I am grateful for all of those), man, if we had just reined ourselves in a bit rather than trying to start up so many different things, well, it would've been a different story I guess.

I repeat, I am grateful for all the lessons of life, whatever they are. You might be thinking, "aye, right, LD!" after the above-mentioned mini-rant, but honestly, I am so grateful. Mostly I'm grateful for having two solid business partners in Alex Robertson and Conar Tracey, as – without them – I genuinely don't know what would have happened, and that is quite scary to think about!

Anyway – back to portfolios...

We've now acquired over 10 portfolios for our own stocks. Some we kept, some we held for a while then sold on. Many, though, outside of our own acquisitions, we have traded on to our clients to allow them to grow at a rapid scale. I think it was in the 12 months of the year 2024 that we traded something like £50m worth of property, and that was only across Scotland. The acquisition of portfolios allows you to scale massively in a single deal. That said, they, like any business venture, don't come without their challenges, but have many positives also.

Portfolio Benefits & Potential Pitfalls

Here's a list of some benefits of portfolio deals:

- Tax relief:
  - The tax treatments are different in different Nations throughout the UK, but if buying 6 or more units in the one transaction, this is classed as a commercial transaction, therefore ADS (Additional Dwelling Supplement) is not applicable.
  - Non-residential rates of SDLT/LBTT also apply to commercial transactions, which are more favourable than the residential rates.
    - SDLT is Stamp Duty Land Tax
    - LBTT is Land and Buildings Transaction Tax (in Scotland)
  - MDR, or multiple dwellings relief, is applicable in Scotland but was scrapped in England in 2024.

- Cashflowing assets day 1:

  - Assuming the portfolio is tenanted, which most of them are, you will have rental income day 1, assuming the tenants are paying the rent!

  - Even using acquisition funding, you will usually break even on cashflow, before refinancing which should increase cashflow.

- No refurb costs front end:

  - Note I mention front end. You may or may not need to refurb properties, but this would be common practice anyway during tenancy changeovers.

  - The point is, no significant cost for refurbs needs to be factored into acquisition cost analysis.

- Expectation of discounts:

  - You're an investor buying an asset from another investor. Investors know the way this game works. Investors are already expecting some level of discount, so you're starting from a discounted position against the assets' true value.

  - You can use the portfolio valuation value (also known as the single asset value) as a starting point for your negotiations, which is often around 20% below the true aggregate market value of the properties.

- Economy of scale on fees:

  - Since only one transaction but with multiple units.

  - Sourcing fees less per unit, generally speaking.

- Legal fees less per unit, generally speaking.

Here's a list of some potential pitfalls you should be aware of and try to combat through the buying process:

- Access difficulties:

  - Access may be required for lots of different reasons.

  - Tenants, likely in situ, can be very difficult to get a hold of.

  - Tenants, even when you do get hold of them, and they do agree to be in the property at the agreed date and time, will fuck off to Asda and will consequently not be in, resulting in the appointment needing to be reorganised.

  - Correct sets of keys to the properties. Existing agents, assuming the properties are not self managed, SHOULD have the correct keys for the properties. However, tenants live in their own little bubbles sometimes and might lose the keys, change the locks, and not bother to tell anyone about that.

- Vendor situation:

  - Usually distressed vendors, for one reason or another, are generally not reasonable people.

  - Last minute, so many vendors change the goal posts and try to mess with the deals.

- Front end costs:

- The complexity of larger transactions means that they could fall down at any point throughout the process, for an infinite amount of reasons.

- You might find, especially if it's your first portfolio or larger deal, that you need to pay your lawyers fees in advance.

- There will likely be requirements for undertakings to be signed, even if you don't have to pay upfront. Undertakings are commitments to pay from the Directors and / or Shareholders of the business.

- Sourcing fees are much larger for portfolio transactions, which must always be paid up front, mainly to give the vendor comfort that there is financial commitment from the buyer to proceed with the purchase of their units.

- Cashflow:

- You will plan things out to perfection, for X amount of cash to be allocated to the purchase within week Y, and for one reason or another the transaction will become delayed, which will push your cashflow allocations out to month Z, which can consequently impact on the acquisition of more deals you have in the pipeline.

- Large sums of cash moving in and out are difficult to control, so you need to stay on top of that, and appreciate that things WILL change as deals progress.

- Acquisition is one thing, refinance is another thing, and at both stages there will be LOTS of fees, and sometimes you are completely unaware of the fees until that last minute, and again this can impact on your overall cashflow.

- Timelines:

  o So many external factors can influence how long a portfolio transaction takes. Sellers get very frustrated when things take longer than their expectations, so it's important to keep rapport at all times, even when things get heated – only if you want to get the deal over the line, of course!

  o Buyers – yes, you – can also become very frustrated as timelines drag on. You might be the buyer or you might be the agent in the middle trading the deal on, but timeline delays are very real, so get good at dealing with the pressure as it comes. Pressure is a privilege, remember!

- Expiring Surveys:

  o Lenders will typically look for a survey dated within the last six months as a maximum timeline. I've seen it time and time again where the deal is due to settle after six months and one week, and the lender insists on new surveys being done, at more cost to the buyer, and more time for everyone, including perhaps another 100% physical access multiplied up by X number of tenants and X number of properties. Do what the lender wants and you'll get the money. Don't do what the lender wants and you won't get the money!

  o As crazy as this might seem, lenders do have a lending policy that they stick to and in most cases are governed by, if they have institutional lender backing which most do, so it's important to respect their positions,

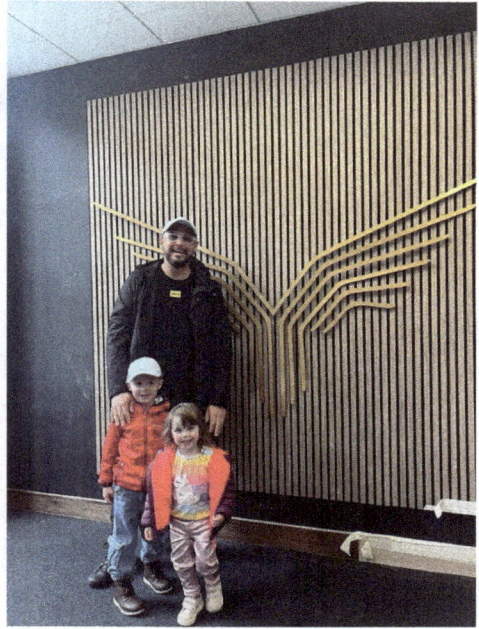

appreciate their perspectives, and ultimately do what needs to be done to get the deal concluded.

Portfolio Due Diligence

Let's take a look at some of the things you should consider when analysing a portfolio deal:

- How many selling entities & the names of those?

  - You should be checking out the number of entities as this can impact on your tax relief position if, for example, you are buying four units from company 1 and three units from company 2. That's seven units in total, but not six or more from the single entity.

- ○ Have a look on Companies House to understand the business(es). You can usually find out some good information from researching the people and the companies.

- Copy of the latest HR(s) / financial survey(s):

  - ○ So many vendors will tell you that they don't have any info on these. If there's finance, there's surveys, and you can check if there's secured finance by the Charges section within Companies House.

  - ○ If they don't want to give you the info that they have, that's a different story, but then you need to understand the reasons why not. It doesn't need to be a deal killer, but it can tell you a lot about the vendors how they choose to answer this question.

  - ○ If the seller has portfolio lending in place, with only one or two commercial funders across their total asset base, there will be a portfolio valuation figure (also known as the Single Asset Value, or SAV), and you can use this to your advantage too, since many funders will only ever lend against that reduced value from AMV.

- Where have the stated seller sale values come from?

  - ○ There are a few different platforms online now that can provide desktop-based valuations from reported data, so that can be a good place to check valuations.

  - ○ You should also always do your own due diligence by using the likes of RightMove for market analysis.

  - ○ Sellers, obviously – and don't lie here, because you would be exactly the same...! Sellers will generally think that their properties are worth more than they are, or at least they will hope / expect that you will buy them for a higher price than what you actually will.

- o It can happen, where the sellers underestimate the property values, and after your research you realise that they are worth way more than what the seller thinks they are, which can be a beautiful place to be when you enter negotiations.

- Are all properties fully compliant with current safety compliance legislation?

  - o Been here, done that, and bought several different T-shirts around this legislation thing. You might be baffled to know that not every landlord keeps their portfolio compliant with safety legislation. I think that is absolutely bonkers, but it is actually very common. Any time you take on any property, if it's being let out, please make sure you have all the compliance documentation in place.

  - o Typically the basics are:

    - Gas safety

    - Legionella

    - Electrical safety

    - Smoke and heat detection

  - o If you have larger properties and are licensed under HMO (House of Multiple Occupation) or STL (Short Term Let (i.e. operating as Serviced Accommodation) legislation, then you will also likely need to consider:

- Fire risk assessments

- Fire alarm system

- PAT Testing (Portable Appliance Testing)

- The licence documentation itself

- Letting safety compliance documentation:

  - There might be documentation, but is it correct, in date, and in line with legislation?

  - Check for missing pages, inaccurate data, or poorly-legible scanned documents.

  - Ensure the engineer is registered with an appropriate governing body.

  - Note if you're doing deals with likes of Councils or Mears, they will insist on particular qualifications and registrations – check with the relevant tenant type to clarify any specifics here.

- Tenancy agreements:

  - Still SATs (Short Assured Tenancies) down south; in Scotland, we have PRTs (Private Residential Tenancies), or there might be a unique tenancy style document depending on the situation and what tenants are in there.

  - If you're buying units that are currently operating as Serviced Accommodations (or "SAs"), you will want to obtain visibility of P&L (Profit & Loss) or income statements from the existing operating agents.

o When you take ownership, you will want to deal with new tenancy documentation, since the new owning entity name will be different from the previous owning entity's name.

o Note all the tenancy stuff should be provided from the managing agents, or the vendor themselves if they are self-managing, and assuming you are not going to self-manage then you should rely on your managing agents to deal with the tenancy docs on your behalf.

- Refurb / upgrade works required - any?

  o If so, what budget value and for what scopes of work?

  o Even if the vendor says the properties are in mint condition and there's no refurbishments required, obviously as part of any tenancy changeover cycle you should be expecting some form of cost to go into that. If no cost, happy days! But that's a bonus situation for you.

  o Sometimes, the existing landlords may not have cared so much about the property, particularly in cases where the tenant has been problematic by causing damages or not paying rents, etc. In these cases you might find the properties are in worse condition than the landlord is even aware of, if they have not been checking in to assess the condition, and if the tenants have had a disregard for their own personal hygiene and living conditions. You might not have a refurb cost initially on this type of unit, but you definitely will have when that existing tenant moves out.

- The applicable sourcing / selling agent fee:
  - Note there could be two fees to factor in, as there could be another sourcer or selling agent involved. This doesn't necessarily mean you have additional fees to pay, since the other person involved might have agreed their fees with the seller, rather than with you as the buyer, but just be aware that this could crop up. You hear a lot about co-sourcing these days – not something we do a great deal of, to be honest, but it can happen.

  - Obviously the deal still has to stack for everyone involved, so usually even if there are two agents involved, the agents will manage the fees directly between them, and you as the buyer should only have the one fee to pay.

- Sight of a selection of photos / video walkthroughs:
  - A seemingly simple request, but it can be like pulling teeth when trying to get a hold of pictures and videos. As the buyer you simply want to have a look around and check general condition, without having to physically travel to the location of the properties and coordinate access arrangements.

  - Obviously if the properties are close by to where you are located, you could take a trip to have a look around the area and the buildings themselves, but you definitely need to see inside, and at least some if not all. You can take a view on the balance of units if you can't see in every single one.

- Be aware that even if you do get sent some, but not all, the vendor is likely showing you the good ones and probably hiding some of the units that are worse for wear!

- Access for OUR (sample batch of) initial viewings – okay?

  - This is front end, before you're even in legals. After you've had an initial look at the pictures and videos, get yourself out to the units and see for yourself.

  - If you really can't make it yourself, have someone you know, love and trust go for you, and they can report back to you.

  - If the vendor won't allow you access, this should raise alarm bells.

- Access for lender surveys during completion process – okay?

  - Now, this stage of the questioning and this stage of the process (if and when you get to that stage) is absolutely critical to the deal going ahead or not. Most lenders will require physical access to every single unit. This process is a task and a half, and is obviously much more challenging the larger the size of the deal you're doing.

  - The good thing is, when you're doing these types of larger deals, you're dealing with the surveyors directly, so you can have a good chat with them before you're even at this stage, to get a much better understanding of where the numbers might land.

  - We've done varying degrees of larger and smaller deals, where we've had anything from 25% physical survey access agreed with the lender, up to 100% physical access required. The less intrusive you can be at this stage, the better, in one regard, since you can reduce the amount of time involved. The less intrusive you and the surveyors are, however, means you see less of the stocks so are taking more of a risk into the unknowns of what has not been physically inspected.

- Are all properties fully tenanted?

  - The general performance of the portfolio should be available in the form of rental statements, but obviously new tenants can move in and higher rents can be achieved from the date the deal is agreed, and equally tenants can move out and some properties may become vacant. Usually, the existing landlord will want to keep the properties occupied as they will have other costs and so will want the income to continue coming in, but we've seen many a case where they prefer not to have to deal with bringing another tenant in for whatever reason.

  - The tenancy turnover thing is part of the property game – just because the properties are fully occupied at the time the purchase was agreed, and the rental value was X at the time the purchase was agreed, does not mean that the properties will be fully occupied at the time of settlement, and you should appreciate the rent may be positive or negative X at that point of settlement too.

  - Even if some units are vacant when you're assessing the deal, it doesn't need to kill the deal off. You might still like the potential of any vacant units. You might think you don't want the vacant units. The vendor might insist that you take the vacant units, or the deal is off. Stay fluid around all this variability – there's no right or wrong – do your due diligence before you make the commitment then it's your decision to make to proceed to purchase or otherwise.

- Bank statements to evidence rental income over last 12 months:

  - This is a very important step. A PDF or Excel spreadsheet is one thing, but having proof from bank statements of rental income being received is essential. Again, vendors might not tell you all the ins and outs – bank statements reveal all (or most, anyway). Of course, they could still skew the numbers if they were intelligent about it, but in the most part the bank statements are the solid evidence you would want to see.

  - Sellers might be resistant to this request, and it will depend on how they have the property business structured. If, for example, they own all their units in their own personal name, and they have their personal day to day banking transactions mixed in to a single bank account (rather than having a separate bank account for all their property related business activity), then they might not want to show you all that. Most people, though, should have a dedicated bank account for their business activity, even if in a personal name.

  - Either way, you need to know what rent will be coming in when you conclude, so your cashflow projections can be accurately analysed.

  - Bank statements should also give you an understanding of maintenance charges. Note that if the letting agent is dealing with maintenance and reducing from rental income, you would need to cross-check the bank statements with the rental statements as well as request the maintenance statements from the existing agent, to analyse all that detail together.

- Details of voids, arrears and maintenance over last 12 months:

  o Most lenders like to factor in a 10% reduction in projected rents received to deal with voids, arrears and maintenance (also referred to as VAM). Depending on the type of stock you are buying, in reality this can be below 5% or it could be as much as 20%! We've seen it all.

  o Note that arrears and maintenance issues can be due to the tenants too, rather than the properties themselves, so bear that in mind. You might have a quality property that's had high levels of arrears and maintenance but no voids. Actually, if you end up having a change of tenant, the performance of that property can drastically improve if they have a positive attitude towards the property, take care of a lot of maintenance themselves (which you might be surprised to know is quite common), and respect the agreed payment terms regardless of what's going on in the property.

  o If there's lots of voids though, that's a different story, and you should be questioning the area, property types, tenant types and general condition of the units. There's a reason if there's a lot of voids, and like every element of this due diligence process, it's not necessarily a deal killer, but you do need to understand the reasons why, so you can take a view one way or the other, once you've consumed that knowledge.

- Any current ongoing costs to be factored in?

  o There might be refurbishments ongoing, in mid refurb, so you need visibility of this.

  o You could acquire a property where there is a high level of arrears and the first thing you'd want to do, probably, is start the eviction process, so you would need to factor in and have visibility of these costs and projected process completion timelines.

  o We've assumed so far that in every case it is the properties being acquired rather than the business that is being acquired, but if it was a business acquisition then there would, no doubt, be various other ongoing costs to factor in such as debt liabilities, staff, vehicles, etc.

  o We will discuss the business acquisition concept in more detail below.

- Any factor fees?

  o Buildings can have common factor and insurance charges, where there is an appointed maintenance company to take care of the communal areas of the property.

  o These costs vary significantly and, depending on what those costs are, it could be the difference between making or breaking a deal. I've seen factor fees as low as £10 per month or as high as £250 per month in some City Centre properties. Depending on what the cashflow looks like before factor fees, you might consider it not worthwhile if they're on the high end.

- o Depending on how many units you own in a block, I've seen lenders insist on a factor being set up, even if all the owners are happy with the normal title allocations for distribution of costs any time an issue arises.

- Any Notices served?

  - o Notices can be issued for a variety of reasons. They are legal documents that require compliance with specific terms. Some of them might include, as examples:

    - Notice to end tenancy.

    - Notice of rent increase.

    - Notice of entry.

    - Antisocial behavioural Notice.

    - Notice of Licence application (for Houses of Multiple Occupancy or Short Term Lets).

    - A Notice of Compulsory Purchase – a "CPO", or Compulsory Purchase Order, is issued from the government to acquire property and land without the owners' consent.

  - o If you're trying to get a deal over the line and the lawyers pick up on the fact there's a Notice served, the lender might not be happy lending until that's been removed, and that could take months. So, if you're in legals and being pressurised to get the deal concluded (and believe me – that happens every single time, no matter what!) then this can cause serious aggro and has the potential, due to unknown time delays, to kill the deal completely from the sellers' side.

- Any Council Tax charges currently being paid?

  - Like all taxation and legislation, this is a moving target, but "double Council Tax" can apply on properties that have been vacant for over 12 months. So if the Council Tax charge is £300 per month when occupied, you as the landlord could be charged double that — so £600 every month, for as long as the property remains vacant.

  - There can be exceptions to this and, depending on the Council region, there has been some varying relief against double Council Tax, but these costs can rack up very quickly if — for example — you buy a portfolio package of six units, but have three vacant units in that list, that the previous landlord never bothered to occupy. You could be liable in this case and have no relief, if the previous owner has already claimed the relief. This could immediately eat up all your cashflow generated from the occupied units.

  - One thing to note is that as soon as you do have a tenant that occupies the property, they would then become liable for the Council Tax charges, and at this point the cost would go back to normal for the tenant (i.e. no double Council Tax for them).

There are a few different things you will want to think about when buying a tenanted portfolio, such as rent apportionments at settlement, as well as a lawyers' retention of rent, for apportionment at a point in time after settlement — usually 30 days is sufficient, but if you have troublesome tenants or a troublesome seller, you might want to extend this retention period to 60 days, to give you more time to make sure all the rent is in fact coming to you and not to the previous owner.

Portfolio Acquisition – Buying the Business

One thing we haven't discussed as yet is the ability to buy the business rather than the properties. As always, there's a lot of pros and cons to this alternative strategy. Buying a business means you will acquire "warts and all"! This means that as well as buying the business – which I have no doubt you consider a fantastic opportunity, as there would be no other reason you've went so far down that acquisition path – and as well as taking on all its undoubted glory, you will also acquire all its flaws. It's a bit like getting married and saying you will love your partner in sickness and in health! Make no mistake about it, buying a business is complex, and there are a tonne of different things to consider – just because the stamp duty is only 0.5% doesn't

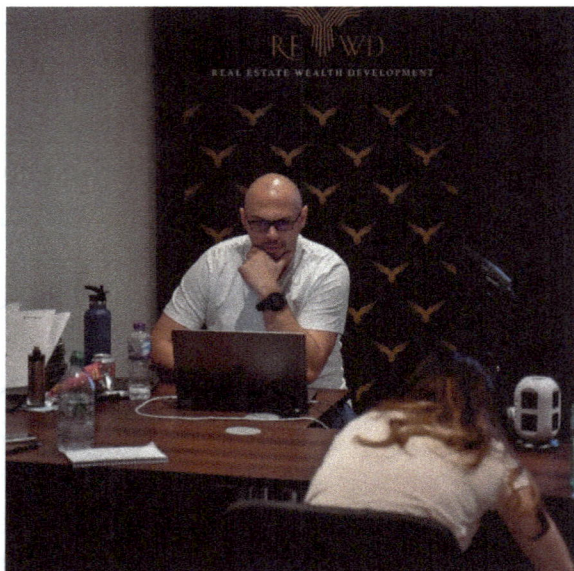

necessarily cut it. Please make sure you consult your lawyers and accountants for an in-depth analysis of all the pros and cons, so you are crystal clear on what you're getting involved in, before you take that leap. Typically, property deals are done on the premise of buying the properties, rather than buying the business, since us simple property investors don't like any unnecessary headaches – we just want to buy properties and let them out, with as little complexity as possible.

Some things you might want to consider if you do have ambitions to go on and buy a business, whether property-related or otherwise:

- Existing liabilities:

  - This could be debts with secured lenders, who would need to go through a lengthy process to even approve you as the new owners in the first place, unless you wanted to change lender during the legals of acquisition.

  - Outstanding tax liabilities of the entity.

  - Ongoing operational costs that have financial agreement tie-ins. This could be for the likes of vehicles, IT hardware, software subscriptions, consultancy contracts, etc.

  - Personally-guaranteed debts from existing owners. Now these, in theory, can be dealt with by counter-guarantees from you as the new owners, but in practice it's likely that in the event of a call up, the lender would claim from the original borrowers first, then the existing borrowers would need to go on to claim from the new owners. A messy process all round – only if it ever was to come up, of course.

- Staff:

  - The good and the bad. The old and the young. Their Contractual Terms. Their personalities. Their attitudes to work. Their ethics. All these people, however many there are, will now fall under your management.

  - Could there be redundancies? Likely you would have to take consultation around how you deal with that, then – depending on the existing staff contracts – there could be additional costs for the business that you have acquired, that could eat into cashflow and profitability.

- Assets:

  - This is a property book, and we're talking broadly about acquiring property businesses, so when we say assets we think of the properties themselves. Thinking bigger though, we would need to consider additional asset classes that would again form part of any business acquisition.

  - Like the cash in the bank! Well, firstly, is there any? If there is, you could factor that bank balance into the deal, however that's structured. How is the vendor planning to deal with the extraction of that cash? If they take it as dividends, they could pay around 40% tax against that. If they were to include it in the sale, though, and you were to pay a higher value to acquire the company, then they could be paid a similar value that might only attract around 20% tax, since the lower rate of tax can apply to the sale of shares (versus cash extraction as dividends at the higher rate). You could get funding against the purchase price too, which could also contribute to your creative flow here.

○ If there is cash, does the vendor even want or need it? If they don't, all in one lump as part of the sale, is there a phased buyout option? Maybe they are paid out over a period of five years, as example, rather than all at once. Could you use the cash in the business to help you grow in the meantime? This is a common exit structure used in the world of M&A (which stands for Mergers & Acquisitions), and – perhaps obviously – you would be expected to align on how that payout is secured for the vendor, if over a period of time.

○ Vehicles. Maybe you don't really want to take on a banged up 20-year-old Mercedes that the current owner has been running around in, that they pay a fortune on continually repairing, for some reason. Maybe you don't want the two crappy maintenance vans that cost the company a grand a month – you'd want to subcontract out the maintenance anyway, surely! So unless you deal with these through the legal process, you would be acquiring these too.

○ These are all thought-provoking examples, of course, but I trust you get the point.

Portfolio Funding

The way portfolios are funded can be very different from single unit acquisitions. The reason for this is that the lenders will typically lend on different parameters of a portfolio – it won't necessarily always be against the total of the combined open market values. I briefly mentioned SAV earlier – SAV is the Single Asset Value of a portfolio. This is where a surveyor will assess the package of units based on a sale in one single transaction. A simple example of portfolio valuation figures could be as follows:

- 10 properties valued at £100K each.

- Total aggregate market value (or the AMV) is then 10x £100K = £1m AMV.

- The surveyor might suggest that if they were to all be sold as one single package, the "single asset value" could be £800K total (i.e. a discount of 20% applied for the sale as a single asset).

  - And I'm sure you will agree that this would be in line with your expectations in terms of discount level for a portfolio deal. Right? Yes, yes, yes! You professional property investor, you. A starting point, always, then negotiate down further from there.

- After the SAV, there are then typically two other values assessed by the surveyor and reported on to the bank:

  - 180-day valuation – this is the expected sale value of the properties, in a single transaction, should a sale be required within 180 days of listing for sale.

    - The 180-day valuation could be around a 30% discount from the AMV (ie. £700K in this example).

  - 90-day valuation – this is the expected sale value of the properties, in a single transaction, should a sale be required within 90 days of listing for sale.

    - The 90-day valuation could be around a 40% discount from the AMV (ie. £600K in this example).

- The summary of all these values is therefore:

  o AMV = £1m

  o SAV = £800K

  o 180-day = £700K

  o 90-day = £600K

There are different things that can impact these values, such as geographical density. This is where, for example, all 10 units are in the one block. Alternatively, there might be two blocks of 5 units each, right beside each other. Another situation could be 10 units, not in the same block, but all in the same street. Then, if you consider a situation where every unit of the 10 is in a different town, well it's difficult to see why any reduction in value would apply, as in the event of a default – if the bank had to list them all for sale at the one time – each unit would have no impact on the saleability of the other. If you think about 10 units all in the one block though, all going up for sale at the one time, this could have a massive impact on 1) the sale price of each unit, and 2) the length of time that each unit would actually take to sell.

We've not used the terminology so far of "portfolio valuation" (or the "PV") but, depending on concentricity of the units in the package being surveyed, this is where we might see a difference between the SAV and the PV. The SAV is suggesting the sale price of the package of 10 units being discounted from the AMV, due to sale as one transaction. The PV may or may not have a discounted level depending on just how concentrated the units are as a portfolio – if they're all spread out in different towns, we would expect no reduction from the AMV in this case. These conditions are for awareness of assessment scenarios and rarely impact on the lending side, since most lenders will consider the 180-day valuation figure. There are lenders out there that will consider all the figures, though, and since the lending market is constantly evolving, it's good to have a base level understanding of all of these terminologies and think about how they may or may not impact on either your decision making for acquisitions, or the lenders from their perspective to lend.

Some of the above-mentioned concepts might be new to you, so make sure you go back and digest that first, before we start to look at the way the lending might work, as again that's very different to how single unit deals might look.

Continuing on with that same portfolio example above, we now need to think about what value the lenders will lend against and why. This does vary massively depending on who you're dealing with, and whether or not they are lending against the portfolio, or only a few of the units within the package of 10. Go with me here though, as this is in fact just an example, but obviously every package, every survey, every lender, and every situation is going to be different. That said, this same principle will apply when you're looking at portfolio lending, so at this stage we will crack on, on the basis that we are using one single lender for lending on the total portfolio as one single package.

So...!

If we think about the acquisition stage – typically we are buying on bridges, refurbing if necessary, renting them out (if not already tenanted), and then refinancing on to term loans, assuming we are working on a BRRR style deal. It's common for lenders to lend against the 180-day valuation figure, as long as there is not more than a 10% variation between the 180-day and 90-day valuation figures. If the variation is larger than 10%, the lender might look to reduce their loan value even further – this simple survey detail has caused us so much aggro in the past, it's unreal. But you're probably thinking "why am I only getting lending against a value that is already heavily discounted from the true values of the properties!?" Simply put, this is how commercial funders view their risk, and simply put, this is how they roll!

Example of how this might look in terms of lender ratio analysis and deposit cash required, could be as follows:

- 180-day valuation figure = £700K

  o Let's assume in this example this is the value you are paying as your purchase price – so a 30% discount against the AMVs, which should be a decent deal in anyone's book!

- Lender LTPP (loan to purchase price) ratio = 80%

- Lender loan value = 80% of £700K = £560K

- Lender LTV (loan to value) ratio = £560K into £1m AMV = 56%

- Lender LTSAV (loan to single asset value) ratio = £560K into £800K = 70%

- Your deposit cash = £700K - £560K = £140K

Note the lender's position, regardless of what value is being assessed, is nice and secure! And that's exactly how they like it.

If you were to purchase for £800K, the lender would likely still lend against the 180-day valuation figure, meaning you might have to put in extra cash. 20% is still a decent discount, so you would just need to analyse the whole deal in its entirety and decide whether or not this was a discount level that was good enough to allow you to proceed with the purchase. We actually have portfolio deal calculators too, to help with this more detailed analysis of total costs required, so again please just reach out if you want access to this and the team can sort that out for you. We've found recently, due to the ever-increasing ADS tax legislation, that buyers seem to be willing to accept lower discount levels due to the tax savings alone. That said, if you managed to secure a larger discount, say 40% – so purchasing for £600K, in this example – the lender (in most cases) wouldn't lend against the 180-day figure, they would likely move their lending to the purchase price and offer something like 80% LTPP, meaning a lend value in this case of £480K. Generally they say they will lend against "the lower of" whatever figures are being analysed.

So I think I've detailed enough here about the principles of portfolio lending and clearly demonstrated the differences between this type of lending versus single unit term loans. It's important that you recognise this section of the book is purely to educate. In reality, there are many different ways we can skin a funding cat! When it comes to 1) acquisition funding, then 2) refinance (or term loan) funding, we always want to assess what options are going to give us the maximum lending value at the cheapest costs, at the different stages in the process. In the current market there are various options for lenders that, in this case, would take on a portion of the units each. For example, for the total of 10 units, you might have 3 units with one lender, a different 3 units with another lender, then the balance of 4 units with a third lender – so three lenders in total, rather than dealing with one single lender on a portfolio loan. The benefits of using different lenders is that effectively each one of them is offering you a term loan (or mortgage, if you want to call it that) on the basis of being a single unit lend, meaning you can usually obtain 75% LTV funding at competitive rates of interest.

An example of how this portfolio could then be funded at point of refinance, regardless of how you acquired, could be as follows:

- 10 units at £100K each

- 10 loans at £75K each

- Total lending = 10x £75K = £750K

I'll let you do the maths to calculate how much cash you have left in the deal, depending on what examples you want to work through yourself, but yes – if you're wondering – this could then be an all-cash-out portfolio deal – and yes, they are out there! We've not even looked at cashflow analysis here either, whether at point of acquisition or refinance, but – yes, yes, yes – this is how to play the game professionally. And while we're on a high,

with pennies dropping all around us, I might as well throw it in here, that no – you don't need any of your own money to do any of what is being outlined!

So go out there and raise some money, buy some deals, repeat the processes over and over again, and get working on this new way of life that you so badly deserve for yourself and your family!

Legals

Lawyers are a breed of human I have come to love and hate. There are some really good ones and some really bad ones. Then there's the slow ones and the problematic ones. It's a really fascinating place to be, in this legal landscape! We've probably been through over 10 different lawyers since we started, leaving each one for a different reason. Now, I'm glad to say, we have a core team of people that we use who work well together and get the job done. We always suggest that our clients should consider using our team of suppliers – known in the property world as "the power team", for some reason. (I've never understood why only in the property space, would you call a supplier a member of a powerful team.) They are your suppliers, you will be their customer, and if you're doing lots of property deals you will be a good, valuable customer to them, and they will want to support you as best they can. Of course, at all times, complying with the Law Society rules.

As one lawyer once told me: "Laurie, I am an officer of the Court first, and a lawyer to you as a secondary."

I obviously wasn't a good and valuable client to that particular lawyer then! We don't do any business with them anymore either, FYI. But, of course, I respect their position.

Anyway, I remember back to doing my first property transactions and I had such a different view of lawyers. I was kind of scared of them a little bit, scared of the process, confused about documentation, concerned about signing stuff. What if I messed something up – would I go to jail?! Lawyers can be thought of as some kind of superior race at the highest point of the hierarchy, when really, they are just people, in business, making a living, practising their trade of law. As I'm sure you can imagine, we have dealt with so many different types of transactions there really isn't anything that hasn't come our way in terms of problems and situations that we've had to overcome on a legal basis. When you're dealing direct to vendor too, these sellers are usually distressed in some way; they're not easy to deal with, and we as the agents in the middle often incur so much heartache just trying to keep everybody in the transaction sweet, to get deals over the line. Nowadays, we have good, solid relationships with lawyers, we know the game inside out, we have good people that we work with, and most of the time we do always get the deals done. It really is only on the very rare occasion that a deal falls apart for some reason. And there's wide and varied dynamic reasons floating around constantly, with the potential of killing deals off.

Since we're covering Legals within the Finance section of this book, I wanted to talk more about what's involved in terms of documentation, processes, timelines and securities, mainly. Believe me, there is no legal scenario we have not been involved in, so we are very well versed here. If you were to summarise our skillsets, we would probably say Legals, Finance and Deals. Depending on your level of experience, you might be better versed in some of these areas than others – but rest assured that after reading this section of the book, when it comes to knowing and understanding what's involved to get deals done in the property world, this should make your life a lot easier!

Also just to point out the different lawyers that would typically be involved in any one single transaction:

- Your lawyer, acting for you as the purchaser (yes, that's you, you property PRO!)

- The seller's lawyer, acting for the vendor, selling the property to you

- The bank's lawyer, acting for your funder, assuming you are acquiring with some kind of funding that requires legal input on the lender side

- An independent lawyer, not connected to the transaction, that will assist you with what is known as ILA, or Independent Legal Advice, which will be required in most cases where there are PGs (or Personal Guarantees) involved

Before we go into documentation requirements, just to talk briefly on the PG requirement again, I try to think back to a point in time where a PG was not a necessary part of lending. Now, apart from maybe some lower LTV products, in my experience, a PG is required every time. Apparently there was a stage in time where banks would lend money to a business, and if the business was going south, the owners could just hand the keys back to the bank and say: "There you go – I'm off, and you can deal with getting your money back after you deal with the winding up of the company!" For me, whilst I know this was a way of operating previously, in my experience to date, every single lender always wants a PG. Maybe that's because I deal in low value, high yielding resi stocks! The PGs create a connection between the borrower (as an individual) and the borrower as the corporate entity, assuming it is a corporate entity that is borrowing, because if you are a property PRO you will likely not be buying in your own personal name. I cannot imagine a scenario where a lender will lend and not insist that you provide a PG. We have lots of different types of funding across our Group of companies, on the investment side and the trading side, and for every loan, there is a PG involved, ensuring all three Directors (that's myself, Alex and Conar) are held personally liable for that debt until repaid.

Documentation

I'm going to list out common documentations required on the legal side and I'll go on to explain each one of them in a bit more detail under each point:

- Security

  - This is the legally registered document on the land register, which creates a Legal Charge. This can be described as an entitlement to the lender to take control of the asset and sell it off in order to recover their debts should they go unpaid.

  - It can be as simple as a one page document or, depending on the lender and situation, into the 10s of pages per single unit. You can imagine the amount of paper involved in a portfolio transaction of even only say 10 units!

  - The only time you will not be required to sign a Security document, would be in a case where you are borrowing funds on an Unsecured basis.

- Personal Guarantee

  - As described above, this connects the borrowers as individuals to the borrower as the corporate entity. If, in the event of default and call up of Security, if there are insufficient funds recovered from the sale of the secured asset, the lender is legally entitled to claim against your personal estate, i.e. your home, your cars, your cash, and your DVD player!

  - PGs freak a lot of people out, but the fact is that as long as you continue to pay the bank you will never have a problem. If you consider that you borrow at say 75% of the true value of the property when you refinance, the bank would need to sell it at say 80% of the property value (so a 20% discount from its true market value) to recover their funds, allowing for costs in this example too.

- ILA / ILA Waiver

  - Every time you talk to lawyers about PGs they will tell you not to sign them. No lawyer will recommend that you sign a legal document that entitles anyone to any of your personal assets. The majority of banks now insist on what is known as Independent Legal Advice or ILA, where an independent lawyer (unconnected to the transaction) sits you down to talk you through all of the reasons as to why you should not sign the PG.

  - Depending on how many deals you're doing, as well as what lenders you're working with, it can be an option (to save time and cost) for you to sign what is known as an ILA Waiver document. This basically just says "I know what I'm signing, I know the risks, I know you want me to take ILA on it, but I've done so many of these that I don't want or need the ILA and I'm happy to sign the PG anyway, accepting all that goes along with it!"

- ○ Usually it would be commercial funders that you have a decent track record with that will allow you to sign a waiver, so you can dodge any meetings or calls around ILA.

- Solicitor Certificate

  - ○ This document is for the solicitor to sign only, to confirm to the other lawyers (and the bank) that they have in fact had the conversation with you, explained the risks of signing the PGs, and you decided to proceed anyway.

- Board Minute

  - ○ The Board Minute document is probably the most mental document out of all these requirements. I can understand the need for the other documents. A Board Minute, I do not understand, especially if it's just you on the company as 100% owner and the only Director. But anyway, you will need to sign this, so it's important to understand what it is and why it's there.

  - ○ This Minute records the fact that you had a meeting – yes, usually with yourself – and you discussed taking out the loan. You then agreed – yes, usually with yourself – that you should proceed in taking out the loan. A worthwhile discussion that should be recorded, I'm sure you will agree!

  - ○ I jest, but ultimately this is another bit of backup for the bank to confirm that there was a meeting, the relevant people to the loan were in fact present, it was on X date at Y time at Z location, taking the loan was discussed, and the decision was taken to proceed with the borrowing. Like I say, if you are the sole owner and Director, it's all a bit silly here, but if there are more people involved in the company than just you, this is really where it becomes relevant to record the meeting for the bank.

It's important to note that you will need to sign these documents with a "wet ink" signature, which basically just means they will not be accepted to allow completion in any kind of electronic form (i.e. a scanned copy or an electronic signature). Usually, although it can be lender-dependent, the lawyers must be in possession of the original piece of paper with the original wet ink signatures (not just the scanned copy by email), before the transaction can conclude.

These documents are the main documents used on every transaction but, depending on how complex the deal is, there can be various other things involved. I mentioned a BFC earlier – the Bond and Floating Charge – known in England as a Debenture. This is where the bank also takes Security over ALL ASSETS of the business – that's properties, cash, IT equipment, vehicles, and whatever else is in there, including YOUR SOUL! So basically, in the event of a default, if the sale of the properties themselves don't recover the total amount of monies due to the bank, they can then legally claim from the corporate estate for any balances due. Again, I reiterate, the chance of this actually occurring is very slim indeed. And anyway, if it were me, and things had gone completely south, I would rather they took the company assets than my personal assets!

I think the only other thing to mention – and again, it would only come up on larger deals or where there were more complex funding structures involved – would be what are known as the Deeds Of Subordination. All this really means is that, if there are other lenders involved – it could be private funders in a JV, for example – the Deeds of Subordination ensure that the bank's monies are always the highest ranking, for the avoidance of any doubt. So in a case of default, the bank will be paid first, with any other lenders involved being subordinated behind them.

Processes

I thought it would probably be worthwhile to briefly chat through the actual process of the legal side, so you can understand what happens first, during, then last, and why each of these processes are essential in the overall legal procedure. The process is known as conveyancing, in legal terms. I've taken some guidance on this section from our good friend and favourite lawyer, Fallon Sara Spencer, who we've worked with since the early days of our property journey, across various different Firms she's worked for. I wonder if she'll ever take the plunge and start up her own Practice?! Fallon has such a strong work ethic and has been instrumental for us in getting so many different complexities ironed out and ultimately getting the deals done, which is all we're really interested in as the property investors. She's a great lawyer for both us and our clients, so if you're looking for a recommendation, I'm sure you'll find her on LinkedIn – make sure to mention that it was me that put you in touch with her, so I can get a free lunch!

As a side note here, I wrote this section a while ago and have come back to it as I was nearing the end of writing the book, to give you a bit of perspective. It's currently 04:28 one early May morning, and I've been up since 3am cracking on with writing this book. Now and again, my mind is diverted to different things we have going on in business, and if I think of something I need to act on it there and then – otherwise I will forget about it and things won't move as fast as they should! There's a lot of checking in on things to keep everything progressing, as so many folk will sit on tasks unnecessarily, which can delay processes and ultimately delay cash coming back into your business. I thought about two refinances going through legals there a minute ago, and so dropped Fallon two emails to check in on both these cases. She replied immediately to both emails to confirm that both cases had already been dealt with a couple of days prior, and we were just waiting on other lawyers involved to respond with the requested info. Another lawyer was actually copied in on one of the emails too, as we were waiting on ILA and PG documents from them.

Here's a screenshot of the email inbox to support the story — as I near the end of writing the book I now need to start thinking of what images I can add in!

Now, I'm not saying everyone needs to get up at crazy o'clock in the morning and work, work, work and all that, but I do find it interesting when there's other folk out there that have the same mentality as me in terms of putting in the extra hours, way above and beyond what is required of them, to achieve results that so many others would not, compared to simply just working the 9-5 grind. We all need our free time, our family time, our me-time, our time with friends and relaxation, and all the rest of it, but Fallon's attitude has always stood out to me. This is just one example I thought would be interesting to highlight here as I'm thinking about it, but seriously, if you are looking for a switched-on lawyer who is on the ball, really gives a shit, goes the extra mile, and just gets things done as they need to be done... give Fallon a shout. There are a few other decent lawyers out there, granted, but I've not met another lawyer like her in terms of her attitude to work and her knowledge and experience. I think she's actually only mid-thirties, too!

So when I think about the next generation of the likes of young Ryan "Ryzo" Retson, Kris "Kristal" Pirrie, and Holly "HLH" Hodgson, these guys are all the same in terms of the way they approach business and their attitudes towards success. In the words of Alex Robertson, "It really is quite exciting!" And if you've not seen that animated GIF of Alex and his ever-expanding excited eyeballs, please make sure you dig back through socials, or drop me a DM – it's one of my very few starred WhatsApp images that I love going back to again and again, any time there's something exciting on the radar! But honestly, I do feel like we are building a solid team of great people – both internally and externally – which can only be good for the REAL Property Scotland business itself, as well as for all our awesome clients who are creating life-changing results, by all working together collectively and constantly going above and beyond to achieve greatness in all that we do.

Anyway – back to the education...

Conveyancing is transferring the legal title to property from one entity to another, or the granting of what is known as an "encumbrance", such as a mortgage. Separate solicitors are needed for the seller, the purchaser, and where necessary also

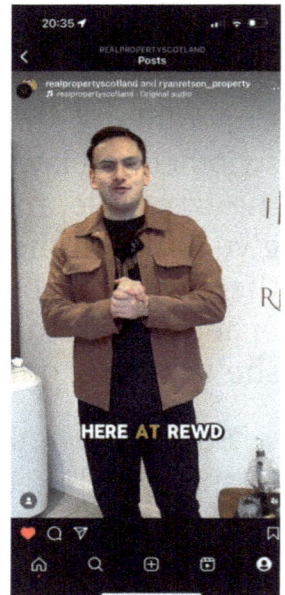

the lender. It's the duty of the seller to provide all documentation relating to the property, such as titles, legal reports, property enquiry certificates (also known as PECs), and any other relevant documentation. The only exception to this is when the seller is selling at auction, where the property is sold as seen. The purchaser's solicitor will then review the documents to ensure that the purchaser will obtain good and marketable title. When there is a lender involved, they will also require good and marketable title to ensure that they have a valid and marketable Standard Security.

The process flow from start to finish is as follows:

- Client Onboarding.

- Purchaser's solicitor submits an offer to purchase to seller's Solicitor.

- Purchaser's solicitor will carry out ID and Source of Funds Checks.

- Seller's solicitor obtains instructions on the offer from the Seller as well as obtaining the relevant documentation.

- Purchaser's solicitor will review documentation to meet the client/lender requirements.

- Purchaser's solicitor drafts relevant documentation for registering such as Disposition, Standard Security and LBTT Forms.

- Negotiate missives.

- Prepare settlement, e.g. updated reports, and submit advance notices.

- Purchaser's solicitor will request funds from the Purchaser and Lender.

- On the Date of Settlement, keys are exchanged for the purchase price.

- All documents will be registered to the Registers of Scotland to update Title.

- The Updated Title Sheet is sent to the relevant parties.

For the paperback readers, here's an image to help you follow that process flow:

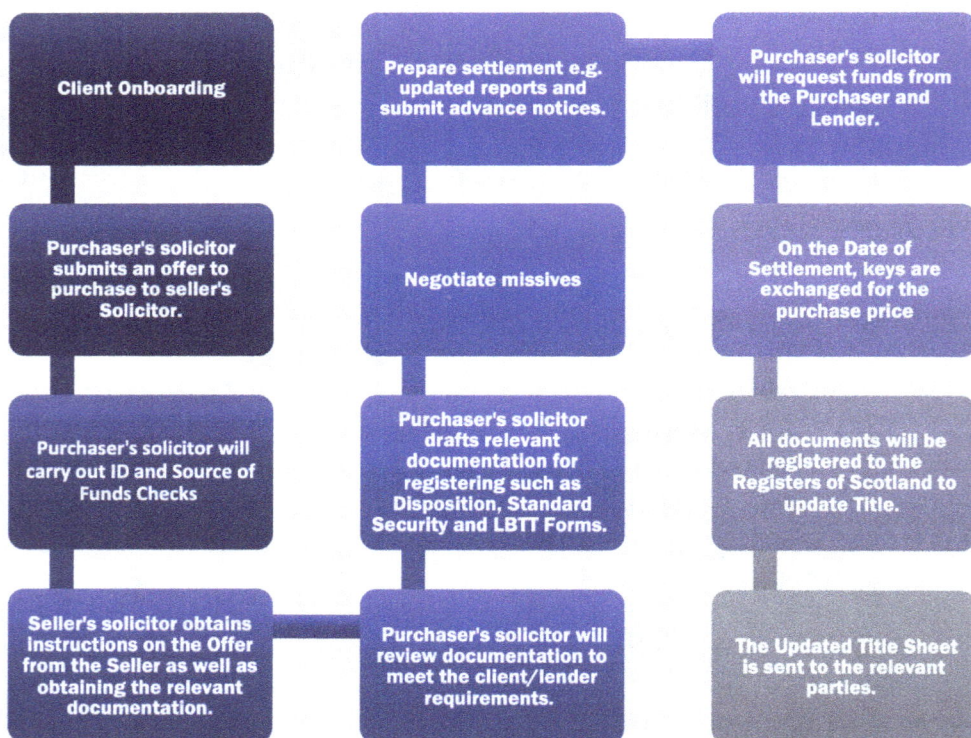

There is another very important part of the Legal process in terms of due diligence which must be performed. Law firms are required under the Law Society of Scotland Rules and Anti Money Laundering Regulations to carry out particular Due Diligence checks. These consist of:

- Photographic ID (Passport or Drivers Licence).

- Proof of Address within the last three months (bank statement or tax bill).

- Where the total amount of money coming into the Law Firm's Client Account is over £5,000, it is necessary to evidence the source of the funds, evidencing how and from where the client obtained their overall of wealth.

There is an old property register in Scotland – it's a chronological list of land deeds from the 1800s. It's based on written descriptions of properties and known as the Sasine Register. If you've ever seen a scanned document that looks like an old scroll, handwritten with a feather dipped in in, then this is probably a copy of an older style Sasine title! The Sasine Register Search Sheet contains a brief description of the property, including approximate size and address or relative location (e.g. 430 out of the 1000 acres of ground bounded on north-west by Edinburgh Road). The property description is followed by a list and short description of deeds submitted for registration. These provide an account of all transactions that have taken place on the property. From these entries it is possible to establish previous owners of the property, price paid information, securities, etc.

Now, time to get geeky... The Land Registration (Scotland) Act of 1979 then created a map-based register of title, and that went live in 1981. There was a process to go through to replace all of the Deeds from the Sasine Register and eventually get all that data on to what is now known as the map-based Land Register of Scotland. It still baffles me to this day, in terms of the number of Sasine titles we come across, but ultimately these are properties that have no need to have their title updated since 1981. Any time there is an acquisition of a property with an older Sasine Title, the property must be registered with the Land Register of Scotland as part of the purchasing process, in order to give a clear updated Title to the new owner and Security to the lender, if there is a lender. Under the Land Register, you are provided with a Title Sheet and Title Plan. The Title Sheet is split into four sections which each outline:

- A) the property boundaries,
- B) who owns the property,
- C) whether there is any security over the property, and
- D) what burdens affect the property.

The Title Plan is what provides the map view of the property.

Sometimes multiple properties can be found on the one title. This can be common with flats and new build properties. We don't necessarily have to, but we make it our own standard practice to split the one larger Title (maybe containing 10 flats, as an example) into multiple different Titles, so that each property has their own Title Sheet and Title Plan. This is beneficial for when it comes to sell and refinance the properties. You tend to find there are a limited pot of lenders that will fund multiple units on a single title, but they will look for a higher rate of interest and will typically lower the LTV offering.

Also, as part of the legal process, there will be three main Searches performed:

- Company Search, including:
  - Company information; for example, registered address, date of incorporation, company registration number, last filed accounts, as well as any other official filings.
  - A list of the current and any resigned officers.
  - Scanned images of any relevant company documents.
  - Information on any existing Charges the company holds.
    - This one is a good way to find out how active people really are, as if they are a serious scaling business, it's likely they will have lots of registered Charges.
    - Good to find out what lenders different people are working with too!
  - Information on any previous company names.
  - Insolvency information, if any.
- Charges Search:
  - For any existing debts secured against any company assets, including a potential BFC against the company itself.
- Director Personal Search, including:

○ Names of owners & directors, appointments, and details of any companies they are involved with.

Any purchase of an "additional dwelling", including a first purchase, by a company or any other type of non-natural person or body will mean that the Additional Dwelling Supplement (also known as 'ADS') will have to be paid. The rate of ADS varies between Scotland and England, so it's always best to check at the time of purchase what taxes will be incurred. Note if the property is below £40K, ADS does not apply. Also, if you are purchasing six or more properties, this would be classed as a commercial transaction (ie. not a residential transaction, even if you are buying residential units), so again ADS would not apply. Multiple dwellings relief (or 'MDR') is available on most transactions that involve the purchase of six or more dwellings in a single transaction, or in a series of linked transactions. The relief ensures the buyer does not pay LBTT at a higher rate than if bought separately and lower rate bands would have applied.

Check specifics of MDR with your lawyers if you're in the process of acquiring a portfolio with six or more properties, and they can confirm the accurate information to you at the time of purchase. It's important to note that this legislation is also variable between Scotland and England, and is always subject to change. There was a time around December 2024, where the government increased the Scottish ADS from 6% to 8% overnight, and − for me personally − resulted in an extra £20K of taxes that were required to be paid as part of the five or six deals we had going through legals at that time. Various clients were also hit with it and unfortunately, as tends to be the case, the sellers were hit hardest, as many buyers simply refused to take that hit and pushed it on to the vendors, insisting the seller must reduce the price relatively if they still wanted the property sold.

Timelines

We've seen deals get done in seven days. From enquiry, to property visit, getting it signed and into legals, on to legal completion within seven tiny little days. Rapid! And if only this was how every deal went. We've also seen deals get done in 3½ years! Yes, you heard me. 3½ incredibly long years. This was the timeline of our longest deal in history, so far, known as "The Aberdeen 100", where we purchased 95 resi units and three commercial units all in the one transaction, without using any of our own money. The assets were valued at £12.5m, we purchased for £7m, and there is a rent roll of around £60K per month gross. Nice deal. Now obviously nobody wants a deal to go on that length of time; anything more than six months – even for a portfolio deal – is just a bit mental. But there are smaller, more straightforward deals and there are larger, more complex deals – and the more deals you do, the more experience you will gain and the more you will learn how to navigate through the variety of incredibly challenging landscapes that can be involved in deals. If we refer back to the Mindset section here for a second – every single time, it will be your mindset that either gets the deal done or doesn't. Remember, you will only ever fail if you stop. So don't stop.

Generally speaking though, we are working on completion times of around 6–8 working weeks for off-market transactions, unless it's a sale under Auction Conditions, where there is a set timeline required for completion. Auction transactions are typically 28 days. Really, we target four weeks settlement on any deal, but usually the vendors are accepting of 6–8 weeks. Plenty time to get deals done! Well, tell that to the lawyers...

From your side, as the property PRO, you need to make sure you've got all your ducks in a row, to ensure that you are not the reason for any delays. Checking, signing and returning documents, both by scanned copies and original wet-ink signed documents by post, always seems to be such a sticking point for people, and something that I cannot understand. Any time we get docs through for signing, it's immediately prioritised and sent back to the lawyers. Sorting out things like your insurance at the last minute also causes delays – there's no reason for this. You should be on the ball and have all this sorted out well in advance of settlement, to ensure you don't lose the deal. Vendors are agreeing to sell their properties at a discount in exchange for a quick, guaranteed sale. If you fuck with that agreement, their typically already distressed state will be heightened, and you will be at serious of losing the deal.

AML (or Anti-Money Laundering) is another one that both buyers and lawyers are terrible for leaving to the last minute. You need to ensure this is all dealt with front end, as in, as soon as your offer goes in. If you are buying under auction conditions, for example, and nobody has thought about AML until the day you're meant to settle, and there's some unforeseen issue that arises that causes a delay, in this case you could lose your buyer fee paid to the auction house, as well as your deposit paid to secure the property, which is typically 10% of the purchase price. The sellers are legally entitled to claim your deposit for your inability to conclude within the agreed timeline.

Some things you cannot be in control of – and there's always a bit of tit-for-tat between the lawyers of buyers and sellers – include each side blaming the other for lack of progress. I've never understood why (for larger portfolio transactions) everyone can't just get round the table, thrash out all that needs thrashed, then crack on to settlement, of course appreciating there is a level of diligence required. There is no need for any deal to drag on beyond six months, and in fact it shouldn't even be as long as that!

Anyway, the point of this section is to highlight potential pitfalls that can cause delays, so you can hopefully improve your acquisition timelines, so you can do more deals.

Securities

We've touched on Securities a bit already in the book, but whatever kind in involved in the deal, you will require a lawyer's involvement to put that in place. A quick recap of likely Securities you will encounter and your funding will be subject to:

- 1st Charge

- 2nd Charge

- Bond & Floating Charge

- Personal Guarantee (PGs)

- Deeds of Subordination

Mainly, you will be required to provide 1st Charges and PGs on every single deal, whether at acquisition or refinance. These are not complicated, so if you're not clear on what they are or how they work, make sure to speak to your lawyer for guidance as required. A 1st Charge allows the lender to claim the property to recoup their monies due, in the event that you default on the loan agreement. A Personal Guarantee allows the lender to come after you and all you own personally, if the 1st Charge for whatever reason does not recoup sufficient funds to repay the lender's loan, interest and any costs incurred due to the call-up of the Security.

Once you receive the Security pack, this means you are close to concluding. Again, thinking timelines, don't faff about with these docs. Simply print them off, sign them all, scan them in, email them back to the lawyers, request to post the originals, the lawyers will confirm the docs are all good, stick them in the post, and you're off to the races now, simply waiting on financial settlement. One point here – I always insist on sending the originally wet-ink signed legal docs back to the lawyers by what is called "Special Delivery" within the Royal Mail post office delivery service. This means the docs will be guaranteed delivery the next day by 1pm, and will be signed for by the recipient. In the past, I've posted stuff 1st Class and it's got lost in the weird and wonderful cyberspace of the Royal Mail network, resulting in more delays and more unnecessary aggro. Usually once it's lost, and assuming the paperwork is time-critical to the deal, which it usually is, this results in me having to print it all off again, getting all signed up again, then drive through to Edinburgh or Glasgow and hand-deliver them to whoever needs them in their possession. It's just not worth it – pay the eight quid odds to use the Special Delivery service – it's worth it. Anyway, you're a property PRO making millions now, what's an eight quid postage charge!?

Phase 1 V Phase 2

Now this is an interesting section of the book to get down into words. The terminologies of "Phase 1" and "Phase 2" were what we used when we first got started supporting others build their own property businesses, and we used them for separating out

what was an amateur buyer from a serious buyer. We were very much operating in Phase 2, when most landlords – even if they had vast experience – seemed to be stuck in what we called Phase 1. It was also very dependent on the lenders being used, their flexibility, and their Terms. It definitely made sense at the time to use these terminologies, but now, since the lending market has changed so much, I would say it has a different kind of relevance.

To try to explain this original concept in a bit more detail, I'll split them into 2 sections here:

- Phase 1:
    - Buying only single units, one by one.
    - Buying only higher value, lower yielding units.
    - Buying only 1 or 2 per month max.
    - Waiting 6-9 months to refinance.

- ○ Restricted to the type of units they could buy.

- ○ Minimal discounts achieved, if any.

- ○ Tying up lots of cash in deals.

- Phase 2:

  - ○ Buying multiple single units, multi-unit blocks and portfolios, all at the same time.

  - ○ Buying anything, including low value, higher yielding blocks of units.

  - ○ Buying 5-10 units per month, plus the portfolios.

  - ○ Refinancing before the purchase had even went through.

  - ○ No restrictions whatsoever on the types of units.

  - ○ Achieving significant discounts, including discounts from the portfolio values.

    - ■ Please refer back to the earlier section of the book to realise the significance of this.

  - ○ Tying up minimal cash in deals, if any.

As you can clearly see, being in our Phase 2 was a completely different place to be from where most (even experienced) investors were operating. We had grown rapidly through Phase 1, had refused to accept that there was not a better way to do it, and had figured out and smashed through into Phase 2, purely from grit and determination to achieve what others had not done before us. This was ultimately how we got from 0-250 properties in only 2½ years, from around 2018-2021. Obviously since then we've diversified a bit and have various different things on the go, now with a solid focus on building REAL Property Scotland, supporting other people achieve what we have, and having an ultimate objective of being the UK's largest homebuyer through our direct to vendor brand of We Buy Homes Scotland.

Back to Phase 1 and Phase 2, with a more current view of this landscape. The main thing to note is that the lending market has shifted massively from back in 2020 when we were really kicking things off. Back then, we would purchase around 5-10 units, maybe into REWD Resi 1 (the 'feeder company') depending on what securities were involved, then move them into our main portfolio company known as 'RWDL' (which stands for Real Estate Wealth Development Limited), and at the same time we would refinance them all together in a bulk refi on a portfolio lend at 70% LTV on a 5-year variable tracker at around 4.3% above base. I've told the base rate saga story already, so you can refer back to that if need be. Note that due to our Group structure we could move units (effectively sell them) into the other company at cost value, therefore wouldn't attract any tax since there were no gains, and the legal costs were marginal, comparatively anyway for this solution back then, which did work a treat for a time. This process would allow us to buy all sorts of units, combine them into one loan, then refinance rapidly, at a reasonable LTV. Now, though, you can obtain 75% LTV at around 6% APR on a five year fixed rate, on single units, no need to package up, with a variety of lenders, which completely changes the game!

What this lending market now allows us to do is effectively become Phase 2 buyers, moving at Phase 2 pace of growth, doing Phase 2 types of deals, but using Phase 1 type finance. Absolute game-changer. If I've not said it before, I will say it now – there has never been a better time to get involved in this property investment game than now – it is absolutely class.

If it's still not sunk in I'll try to elaborate on it a little further, and I guess we can use our largest deal to date, the "Aberdeen 100" as an example, to hopefully give you clear perspective on our strategy for that deal and the processes involved...

So, you buy 100 units, with all units contained in blocks – so call it 10 blocks of 10 units each, for simple numbers. The reality of our deal is different, but this will be easier to explain and the procedure and allocation of units per lender is the same, of course always subject to the lenders' criteria and exposure limits. If you want the specific ins and outs of that deal, drop me an email and I can send you the refinance tracker spreadsheet we're working off, now with around 60 units of the 100 units already refinanced, as we continue to work through the balance.

Anyway, in this example, lender 1 comes in and takes five units per block, meaning they have taken 50 out of the 100 units. Subject to valuation, which you get free in most cases anyway at the time of writing. So costs out have been marginal, only incurring legals and termination costs of existing finance in place that was used for acquisition. Lender 2 then comes in and takes three units per block, resulting in 80 units now refinanced out of the 100. For both Lender 1 and 2, by the way, they are funding at 75% of the open market survey value, which overall I reckon will come out at about £11m overall (versus the £7m purchase price), due to the nature of the Aberdeen market right now. We love the Aberdeen market, if I've not mentioned already, and expect a massive hike in those prices as a correction between 2025 and 2030 – watch this space! In terms of your refi strategy, you now have 20 units left to refinance. Enter Lender 3, that for whatever reason only gives you 65% LTV on the remaining units, maybe since that package is of lower value assets and the lending criteria dictates their policy is such — call it 65% LTV at 7% APR, as an example. Well, I hope you can follow that now we've refinanced all units, at an overall position of something like this:

- Refinance batch 1 = 50 units = 50% of the combined open market value total of £11m:

    o £11m * 50% = £5.5m of value.

    o £5.5m @ 75% LTV = £4.125m new debt level.

    o Equity position = £5.5m − £4.125m = £1.3m.

    o Refinance batch 2 = 30 units = 30% of the combined open market value total of £11m:

    o £11m * 30% = £3.3m of value.

    o £3.3m @ 75% LTV = £2.475m new debt level.

    o Equity position = £3.3m − £2.475m = £820k.

- Refinance batch 3 = 20 units = 20% of the combined open market value total of £11m:

    o £11m * 20% = £2.2m of value.

    o £2.2m @ 65% LTV = £1.43m new debt level.

    o Equity position = £2.2m − £1.43m = £770k.

The result of these three refinance batches is then the combination of the new debt levels of £4.125m + £2.475m + £1.43m = £8m. Note our original purchase price was £7m. Then, if you allow entry costs of £300K and exit costs of £300K, which is over-egging it a little but allows you to see the point, this would mean the total associated costs of the acquisition and refinance were £600K. Total costs were £7m + £600K = £7.6m. Total cash back from refinance = £8m. Net result of £8m − £7.6m = £400K cash in the bank whilst we retain ownership of the portfolio, with an equity position of £1.3m + £820k + £770k = £2.9m. We can assume the 60k per month gross rent is creeping up over time and the cashflow before voids, arrears and maintenance remains relatively similar even with the increased debt level. This similar cashflow is due to the interest rate at refi coming down compared to the acquisition rate, as well as the rents increasing. Overall, between the acquisition and the refinance, you should have created a more efficient and effective performing property portfolio.

I hope I'm not bamboozling you here and it should all make sense, but as always, if you need to check or clarify any point, please simply reach out to me by email or via socials, and we'll do our best to help you get the information you need to allow you to create MASSIVE SCALE for your own business!

MULTIPLE STREAMS OF INCOME

Synergistic Group Businesses

I think it's important to recognise that, in principle, I am sure that everybody would like to have multiple streams of income. The words themselves – multiple streams of income – just sound exciting, with the image created of all this money flowing into your bank account from all these different places. Well, you might have noticed that throughout the book, any time I've referred to "passive income", this term has always been in quote marks. The reason for this is even the most passive of passive income requires a bit of graft to 1) make it in the first place, and 2) keep it flowing in! Like I mentioned earlier on in the book, I don't have any regrets over our journey, as it just wouldn't be the same if it wasn't for the path that's come before us, but I do think it's so, so important to stay grounded and level-headed when you're getting into business, especially for the first time. There's so many crazy ideas we had at the start, that if we had some kind of mentorship from someone a bit further on in their own journey, I have no doubt we would have been counselled into taking different decisions.

Anyway, I guess that now we can be grateful for all of that journey, since we've ended up in a really nice place with multiple synergistic group businesses. We have the buy to let properties on the investment side, we have the developments' business that we use for straight auction flips and refurbishment flips, and we have REAL Property Scotland for support to others growing their own property businesses, including mentorship, off-market deal trading and project management of refurbs. The last entity to add to the mix, which we've still not managed to get off the ground yet, is REAL Finance Scotland, where we want to become the acquisition funder, with the ability to loan up to 100% LTPP, effectively as the private investor, or the bridging company – having the finance company up and running should make a decent return for us, but it should also create a much smoother experience for our clients buying the off market deals, as well as the vendors selling the off market deals. Hopefully we would see some spin-off business across the rest of the Group too.

We have nearly kicked off the finance company multiple times with different potential funders, but at the time of writing we've still not managed to do it. Really, we require a minimum of £2m funding from someone that gets the model, likes us and the Group, and can get comfortable with the Security level. We're suggesting £2m starting point, but the reality is that we would lend that out very quickly, likely within a couple of months. However, our objective was to prove the model before seeking more capital to grow this business, with the expectation of around a £5m loan book towards end of year 1. Maybe there's someone out there reading this book that wants to get involved?! Well, if you've got the liquidity, the appetite, and a similar mindset to us, we'd love to hear from you! As always, drop me an email if that's you.

Our lead generation vehicle of We Buy Homes Scotland does the job of bringing in all the leads from the vendors looking to sell. We then have multiple options for that vendor:

- Buy it ourselves to add to our rental portfolio

- Buy it ourselves to put immediately back through the auction

- Buy it ourselves to refurbish and sell on the open market

- Trade to an investor client

- Sell via auction

- Sell on the open market

Having these options, these multiple synergistic businesses, or our multiple streams of income (however you want to term it), gives us the ability to monetise the leads we receive in all these different ways.

Starting, Systemising, Scaling, Repeating

The startup phase of a business is always the hardest part. There's a lot of people out there that focus on acquiring businesses once they are up and running, as it's way too much of a pain in the arse to get things started up and prove the model works in the first place! The reality of the situation, for most startups, is that the concept of the model is usually wrong, it will fail, and it's only through the constant battle of figuring stuff out that leads to the profitable, successful business that ends up being the model that's gravitated to. It takes a lot of mental toughness to be figuring out problems on a daily basis, whilst still trying to generate revenue. There's so much that needs to change as a business grows – I am honestly delighted to be at the stage we're at now. I can't even imagine writing this book until reaching this stage in business, as I'm coming at it from such a different viewpoint now.

Our revenues over the last six years in REAL Property Scotland were:

- 2019-2020 @ £27.5K

- 2020-2021 @ £43.5K

- 2021-2022 @ £195K

- 2022-2023 @ £376K

- 2023-2024 @ £1.35m

- 2024-2025 @ £2.1m

Even in those last few years of this business, there have been so many changes at a time of constant growth, which has led us to this point now of having a sustainable, proven model for growth, and we are now focused on that with a clear plan of attack. Back in 2020, though, to only do £27.5K of revenue – I can't even imagine the business and operational activities at the time! That is just NOT a business. I don't think anyone could operate on that turnover. Maybe unsurprisingly, that was a loss-making year. Same deal in 2021 – only £43.5K of revenue. It's not a business – albeit we did actually make a profit that year! It's only really through the battles, through continually fighting through the problems every single day, day after day, that we have morphed into the animal that we are now. As you can see, from 2022, we actually started getting somewhere, and really over the last couple of years we have witnessed some serious growth. That's because we have a great team, between Alex, Conar and myself as the owners and Directors, as well as some key individuals in our management team, such as Ryan "Ryzo" Retson, Kris "Kristal" Pirrie and Holly "HLH" Hodgson, who have all been with us through all the challenges and continue to win, with such solid work ethics. Our revenue target for the 2025-2026 financial year is £3.2m. Watch. This. Space.

So we started up, we continually systemised with software, staff, procedures, targets, and distribution of clear roles and responsibilities amongst the team. We have clearly scaled the business, as can be seen from the revenue growth values over the years. Now, it's time to repeat that process! Starting, Systemising, Scaling, Repeating.

Currently we're only operating the full model in Scotland but the next obvious move for us is to start to look at the English market, where we are actually operational as Town & Country Property Auctions, albeit only within the East Midlands area at this time. I would hope that within this year we are able to start replicating other parts of the full model down south. We do actually have multiple clients south of the border already that choose to work with us because the returns are far greater than what can be achieved in England, in most areas. It's quite interesting looking at the buy to let market there – every area has its own little economy going on. Of course, there are pros and cons of the English market, as is the case with any market, but a lot of what we've seen so far – certainly from the East Midlands area, as well as any major cities – is that the interest rate and voids risk is really high due to higher property prices and usually higher debt values, if we're talking buy to let.

For example, if a property in Scotland is valued at £100K, and it's mortgaged at 75%, it will have a debt value of £75K. That's £75K @ 6% APR / 12 months = £375 per month interest cost. The rent in this example would be around £750 per month, which is typical for a two bed flat in most areas of Scotland, but even higher rents in some places too, even for properties of that £100K value. Comparatively, for a similar property in England, the value might be say £200K, so the debt value at 75% in this case would be £150K. Therefore £150K @ 6% APR / 12 months = £750 per month interest cost. So even if the rental income in England was £1K per month, really the risk is much higher, as you're paying out 75% of the rental value in finance costs, before voids, arrears and maintenance, which doesn't really leave you much room for making any money. I appreciate some people will view the lower yielding properties as better stock, as they'll consider (or expect) higher capital appreciation in lieu of cashflow. Well, each to their own, but I'm a money in the bank kind of guy! And capital appreciation just kind of happens in the background anyway, as is demonstrated over the years from all the historical graphs on property price growth. If we compare that to the Scottish property, then, the £375 interest cost into a rental income value of £750 is only 50%. If the English property is vacant, it costs you £750 per month. If the Scottish property is vacant, it costs you £375 per month.

We're biased, obviously, both on lower value, higher yielding Scottish investment properties, as well as from a liquidity perspective, as you can buy so many more units in the Scottish market with the same amount of cash. More units should equal more cashflow, and at less risk – I am a happy man! Noting here that this is even before we've bought at discount and refinanced to recycle our cash. I am sure by this point in the book you have a full understanding of the glorious model we operate with. Repeating the process of a proven model really is very satisfying to do, whatever model that is.

I've given examples of how we've grown our own business here, but hopefully you can relate this to your own business concepts and you get some kind of takeaway from the different points of view discussed.

Mergers & Acquisitions

There is a massive surge in interest for residential portfolio acquisitions now, due to the changes in LBTT (Scotland) or stamp duty (England). So many people are drawn to portfolio deals simply because of the tax savings. Obviously there are other potential positives too, such as day 1 cashflow, not necessarily any immediate refurb costs, instant equity, economy of scale on costs as well as rapid increase in size of your business from one single transaction. In England, the government actually scrapped MDR (which is Multiple Dwellings Relief) on 1st June 2024. In Scotland, it remains in place, for now. Another way to achieve tax savings is to acquire the business, as was discussed earlier in the book. These deals are more complex though, and "warts and all" is not for everyone! Even if the applicable tax is only 0.5%

of the transaction value, which can be the case for stamp duty on the acquisition of a business, there's so much more to consider.

When we had the building company, we aggressively tried to scale that in so many different ways, to try and get the thing operating profitably. We were doing our own Group refurbs, refurbs for our investor clients, our larger developments, architect referral work, kitchens and bathrooms, homeowner extensions and conversions, windows and doors, and anything else you can possibly imagine that has any kind of building work involved! It was an absolute shambles of a time – our worst experience of business, to date. The thing that made that whole experience worse, apart from the staff tradesmen of course, was our decision to acquire another business with the intention to expand the company. We did a deal with a guy to acquire his existing business, to expand on the home renovations side, with him to stay on and work for the business as a sales consultant, but we would take over the management and day to day running of all the operations, allowing the vendor to simply focus on sales and receive his commissions. He would sign up new business (regardless of costs and profitability expectations), get paid his commission in seven days of the sign up, crack on to the next sale, then leave us as the operational business to try to make any kind of money on the job.

Well, what a mistake. Our biggest mistake in business, and that's saying something when you consider all of what we've been through. This is a perfect example of why you must not "get into business with any Tom, Dick or Harry". The relationship between us and the vendor became very sour, very quickly. The existing staff base, that all got on well with each other, all hated this guy we bought the business from. There was a clear disconnect between this guy's personality and the rest of the team, including us as the three Directors and owners of the rest of the Group operations. In the end we had to terminate any relationship we had with this guy. He then went legal on us, and then – after six months of back and forth – refused to come to any kind of settlement arrangement through the dispute resolution process of litigation. After multiple times of expecting to come to an agreement for settlement, he refused to settle for the previously agreed figure, and ultimately forced us into a corner where we had to proceed to a stage of the legal process called Proof. This is basically where the legal action goes into Court, and the costs start racking up – typically around £40k of costs once you get to this stage. The building company was already struggling to hit revenue and profitability targets, had around £250K of other creditor liabilities, and the actions of this guy actually forced us into an insolvency position. That was always a crazy situation to me, and it clearly demonstrated his lack of experience in business. He must've somehow thought that by forcing us to shut down the building company, that he would be winning in some way. The reality is that if you set up your corporate operations correctly, like we had done in our Group structure, each individual entity is protected in these eventualities. So from a position of this guy getting a decent payout, he actually ended up getting absolutely nothing. Maybe a bit of confused false pride that he shut down the building company, but I really don't get it. We never did see eye to eye! Maybe I'm missing something; I must be. Anyway, we engaged a liquidator, they dealt with the shutdown of the building company, and we just cracked on with doing what we do best – buying properties at discount and helping others build their property businesses.

The M&A (Mergers & Acquisitions) thing was a very interesting first experience for us, and it's something we are not put off by from the experience of that first deal that went south. I think the potential is there to really scale massively by adding other existing entities into the Group fold. We would come at it from such a different perspective next time, though. We always have our finger on the pulse for other opportunities that might come along and make sense for us, so will never say never to M&A. If you're new to this strategy, though, and you're thinking of making a move, one thing I would suggest is to ensure you have a solid team of experienced professionals behind you.

We are very lucky in REAL to have the sensationally talented Mr Alex Robertson, with such a vast range of experience, professional analytical prowess, and logically-thinking balanced mind, to help us internally on a daily basis to assess and decide on the best way forward, decision by decision, M&A related or otherwise. Where many businesses would have to request support on the corporate analysis from outside people or companies, which takes time, adds cost and provides a view from an external standpoint (rather than internal, as the business owner), we can very quickly (and accurately, thanks to Alex) review and decide on the appropriate course of action to move the business forward. This is no different to deal analysis on single unit or portfolio property deals, and gives us an extra layer of efficiency which I really do believe has given us the edge over others. Of course, having external advisors – and good ones at that – is also absolutely critical to decision-making on more complex transactions, as external perspectives are also very worthwhile. Even if you don't agree with them, it still gives some pointers to debate over, to really challenge the thought processes and make sure you definitely do want to proceed with whatever the opportunity might be. As I write this, I do feel more full of excitement for our next M&A opportunity – I wonder what it will be! The overall experience certainly can't be any worse than our first! Watch this space.

Staff

Now then! Staff. Humans. Emotional beasts. Complicated beings. But every one of us, so beautiful in our own special way! Humans absolutely fascinate me. Such complex varying degrees of personalities, all with different viewpoints based on a wide range of belief systems. Some easily offended, some cutthroat-focused on achieving results, some completely unemotional, some aggressive, some quiet, some loud... How is it possible to bring an eclectic mix of humans together, to have everyone working towards the same goal, in peace and tranquillity...? Well, I don't think it is! Ha ha.

For some reason, I got landed with all the HR stuff that goes on in our business. Contracts, holidays, hirings, firings, consultations, meetings, absences, statutory sick pay, compliance with constantly changing legislation – it is such a drain on time, when ultimately we are trying to grow a monster property business, where we want to focus on revenue generation and profitability. Whilst I appreciate it is a necessary part of business, and if you want to massively scale you will need a staff base, it really does take up so much of my time. We have made moves recently to offload some of this workload to a new staff member, and I really hope that all goes to plan.

Depending on what type of business you are creating, the likelihood is that having some kind of staff base is essential. I've come to realise that all these HR-related tasks and all the time it takes up, is all just part of the business game. When we first got started out, I remember saying to Alex (back in 2019) that I was so excited to never have any staff. I loved the thought of just working at home, wheeling and dealing, doing our own thing, buying property deals, with no one to answer to and no one to have to deal with, apart from each other and external suppliers that would be grateful for the business we were putting their way. I guess, like many things, our perspective on staff has changed massively throughout the journey. We're now at a point where we have created our own "football team", to refer to the analogy we've been using between the three Directors recently as we try to refine our staff base. We have a set number of positions, certain departments and certain roles, and these roles require to be filled – we don't want any more or any less than what we have now outlined, or so we think at this moment in time! We've had many long, detailed discussions over a very long period of time now to try to get our business to the status of a well-oiled machine, and by creating this "football team" and the one out one in policy for the staff and their positions, has allowed us to get clear on the direction we're heading. Again, if I go back to when we started up back in 2019, we wanted a business for this and a business for that, and liked the sound of idea XYZ... so yeah, why not? Let's create a business for it! It was mad. Now, we know what works, we focus in on that, and the team is clear.

It's also fair to say we've chopped and changed our ideas of these positions over time. I'm not sure anyone can ever get it right from the word go, so I don't regret any of these decisions, as always it's a massive learning curve and the journey wouldn't be the journey without all that has went on in the journey! Different businesses require different make ups of these "football teams" and that's another reason you really need to get laser-focused on what you want to do, as you can spend so much time looking for people that end up being an absolute shit-show of an employee... and that's just the ones that actually turn up for work! Even if we use a professional recruitment agency, it doesn't seem to make a blind bit of difference. The number of people that do a great interview, talk the talk, look the part, show us all the right signs of being someone that could really grow together with the business, a lot of the time, in fact

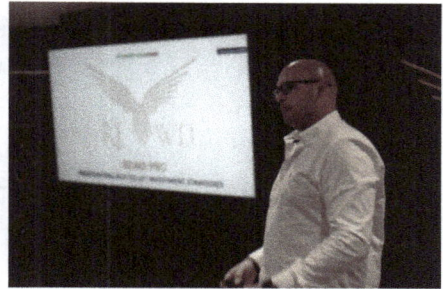

most of the time (in our experiences to date) are a complete waste of time, unfortunately. I really do not understand the human race when it comes to work ethic. I fucking LOVE getting up early and getting stuff done, achieving goals, going above and beyond, learning new skills, writing books, getting up super-early, thinking of new cool ideas and taking actions towards the implementation of those... and it's really sad to me to see so many other folk just go about life doing the bare minimum, preferring to sit around the house and watch TV all day rather than do something constructive! But hey – you are reading this book, so you are in the minority of us humans that actually want to go out there and make something of themselves. Fair play to you, and I wish you all the best of luck! Don't get caught up in this lazy bastard society that we seem to live in within 2025 – there's so many people that can drag you back down into that way of life, if you let them. Want to get around a group of ambitious property investors, doing life-changing deals on a regular basis? Hit. Me. Up.

Growing Pains

Every business will suffer growing pains – it is one seriously crazy ride, and one that is like no other you will ever encounter if you are in fact brave enough to sack off "normal working life" and make a go of it. Number one thing to get right on every single occasion is mindset, of course! First, though, you need to actually get started working towards whatever it is you're going after. So, so, so many people will never even get started, all down to FEAR. That is, False Events Appearing Real (F.E.A.R). Fear holds everybody back. It's been responsible for dream-shattering since time began. It held me back for years. I think most people will say that they wish they got started sooner, if only they knew then what they know now. Well, if you start, you will learn, then you will know. If you don't start, you will never know, so you can't even compare one situation to another.

Letting go and moving on are two things that I've had a massive realisation about over the years. There's a lot of things that will happen in business that are completely outwith your control, and whilst I believe it is important (in fact I would say actually it's essential) that you take 100% responsibility for everything that goes on in your life, there are so many external factors that can influence your operating environment day to day. Other people are entitled to take their own decisions on their own aspects of business and life – if they impact on you, then that's just the way it is. The way you choose to react to whatever that situation is, is on you, and this is where you can step in, take some responsibility, and take your own actions to support your own objectives, but their decisions are theirs to make. I think letting go is a skill that can be learned. I've not always been good

at that. Now, though, I tend – in most cases, and yes sometimes (depending on how big the issue is or was) I need a week or two – to let my mind go through all the motions of the circumstances as I try to get all the different perspectives together to finally arrive at the outcome of letting it pass by, so I can get back to focusing on the main priorities of the business again. It might not be business, by the way – it might be just life, the complicated bitch that it is! I find that I go through the same mental process to deal with the processing of information. Again, it's been a learned thing over the years, but before I was even aware of that process going on, I would allow my emotions to control me, rather than me controlling my reactions to those emotions. I'm getting very "mindsetty" at this part of the book, but I do think these points are really important to mention, as you either allow this "growing pain" (whatever pain that happens to be today) to take over and output certain actions or reactions, or you allow it the time to process, to pass, for you to let it go, so you can move on and get your head back in the game, from a clear standpoint.

You're going to have problems when you try to achieve a big goal. It might be property-related. It might be business-related. It might be relationship-related. It might be health and fitness-related. It might be finance-related. The bigger the goal, the bigger the problems that will come your way. Yin and Yang, man! It's just the way these universal laws work. Embrace it and enjoy yourself along the way. Love what you do and it won't feel like work, even throughout all the heartache and pain. Remember, these are GROWING pains – focus more on the growing and less on the pains. Remember why you set your goals in the first place – you have the opportunity to create a better life for yourself, in whatever regard you choose. That's worth a bit of pain, in my book.

CONCLUSION

Let me summarise... RAISE MONEY, BUY DEALS. It really doesn't need to be more complicated than that. Obviously you might want a bit of help and support along the way, and for anyone interested in that, drop me a DM and we can set up a call. Learn to become better at dealing with the problems, and that will serve you very well. Put it all together and there, my friends, you have a property business.

As the book now draws to a close, I guess I would like to express my gratitude for everyone involved in this journey – that's everyone in the past, everyone current, and anyone that will come along in the future. I express this gratitude to all the good and the bad experiences we've encountered along the way. I know there's so much cool shit still to come out of this crazy thing called life, and I'm excited to see where we go next. I'm not naive to think there won't be more problems and I know for sure that every time one comes up we just get better and better at dealing with them.

I could not have done this (that's the journey and the book!) without the love and support of my totally super-awesome wife Emma – together, we really do make a great team. She takes such good care of me and our family, to allow me to crack on with all my crazy life and business endeavours. We live such an amazing life together with our two absolutely sensational babies, Daniel and Chloe, who naturally give us so much pride and joy. Every day, just watching them grow, is like nothing else I can describe. We are so lucky to have such a beautiful family. I am so massively grateful.

The two main men of REAL Property Scotland and all that is REWD Group, Mr Alex Robertson and Mr Conar Tracey, are absolute superstars. Two guys at the top of their game. It is such a pleasure and honour to work with these talented guys. There is absolutely no doubt whatsoever that we would not be where we are today if it wasn't for these amazing examples of human beings. I am privileged to call these men my close friends and business partners. Together, we really are creating something special. If you want to go fast, go alone. If you want to go FAR, go together.

Throughout this book I've tried to give you a tonne of education, with real life examples of deals, situations, stories, with all the good bits and the bad. I really hope you've taken away massive value. The stuff we do on a daily basis really isn't complicated, and anyone can do it – you just need to believe in yourself and take the necessary actions to move you towards your goal. We are prime examples of that. I would love your feedback on what you think of the content put together here, and really hope and look forward to meeting up with you in person sometime soon too.

Now it's time for you to put all this knowledge into action.

Laurie.Duncan@realpropertyscotland.co.uk

ABOUT THE AUTHOR

Laurie Duncan began investing in buy-to-let property back in 2010, acquiring his first investment simply because it was across the road from where he bought his first home (it had been on the market a while, and he got a good deal on it, of course!). Since then he's been building his own portfolio, as well as that of REAL Property Scotland, and he has been helping others get involved in property right from the beginning.

Laurie has over twenty years' experience in international sales and business development, with a track record of building both top and bottom lines, to enable business expansion into new markets and product ranges. He is constantly seeking out new potential to push the company on to new areas and opportunities.

Laurie focuses on helping clients grow their portfolios with smart strategies and real support. His strength is spotting new opportunities and turning them into long-term wins for the people he works with.

FAST-TRACK TO PROPERTY MILLIONS

By Laurie Duncan, Alex Robertson and Conar Tracey

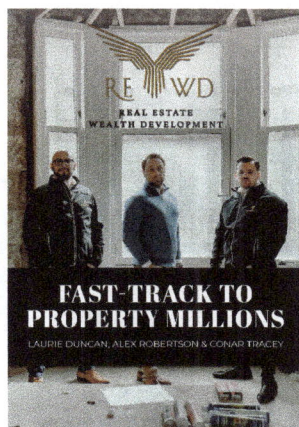

Real Estate Wealth Development, better known as the REWD Group, is one of Britain's most exciting and successful property development companies. Their ambitious vision is to create generational wealth for their key stakeholders by addressing the significant imbalance between supply and demand which exists within the UK property market. Since the business was established in 2018, it has built a multi-million pound residential rental portfolio, converted many empty commercial properties into residential housing including Houses of Multiple Occupation, created brand new properties, and refurbished and/or renovated empty and uninhabitable homes in order to provide additional high-quality stock for the rental market.

With a current undersupply of four million homes in the UK housing market, and an estimated one million homes currently empty throughout Britain, there has never been a better time to be involved in the fast-moving property industry. In this book, the aspirational directors of the REWD Group share their expertise and offer the essential knowledge required to succeed in the world of property, covering topics which include legislation, taxation, due diligence, mindset, finance strategies and much more besides. Drawing on their own remarkable business journey so far, they provide practical examples of how to get started in the property market, moving from the basics through to the detailed strategies you will need to negotiate your own property deals for the first time.

For details of new and forthcoming books from Extremis Publishing, including our monthly podcasts and regular newsletter, please visit our official website at:

www.extremispublishing.com

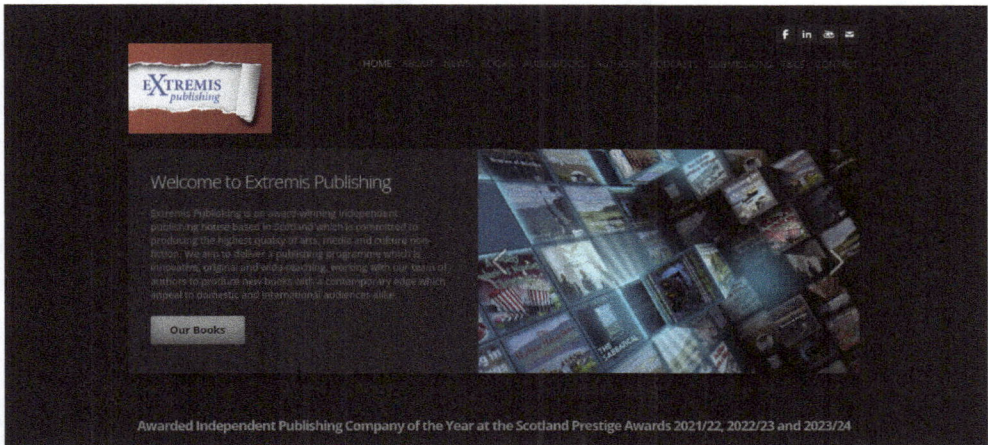

Awarded Independent Publishing Company of the Year at the Scotland Prestige Awards 2021/22, 2022/23 and 2023/24

or follow us on social media at:

www.facebook.com/extremispublishing

www.linkedin.com/company/extremis-publishing-ltd-/